Giuseppe Zanini

The book of
WHY

TREASURE PRESS

Contributors:
Andrea Bonanni   Pinuccia Bracco
Glauco Pretto

Text adapted by
Christine Casley

First published in Great Britain in 1986 by
The Hamlyn Publishing Group Limited

This edition published in 1989 by
Treasure Press
Michelin House, 81 Fulham Road
London SW3 6RB

Text copyright © Arnoldo Mondadori Editore, Milano, 1973, 1986
This edition text copyright © The Hamlyn Publishing Group Limited 1974, 1986
Illustrations copyright © The Hamlyn Publishing Group Limited 1974, 1986

ISBN 1 85051 372 4

Printed in Czechoslovakia
52113/3

INTRODUCTION

Never before have children had at their disposal such a wealth of information regarding the world around them. Never before have books, radio, television and magazines provided the young with such a flood of pictures and news regarding men and matters, surroundings and activities, the present and the past, worlds near and far, and yet never before has the thirst for knowledge been so great.

The more windows we open on the world and the more new horizons are revealed, the greater the demand, for knowledge becomes. We want to discover the reasons behind facts and figures, to reflect upon geographical, historical and scientific factors and their relationships which determine our present human condition.

Children have an inborn desire for knowledge. It is a vital need almost as great as food, play and rest. The aim of this book is to meet this demand in a varied and pleasing manner, to fill the quiet, unoccupied moments of the day. It is a book to be picked up and dipped into as a change, a relaxation.

Behind the deliberate lack of apparent order, relieved only by the division into chapters and units, there lies the intention to provide an assorted collection of informative articles, far removed from encyclopaedias, text books and treatises.

This is a book designed for relaxation but not for that reason devoid of factual information, a book to browse over and to read at random following the whim of the moment, and yet a book which can, if required, become a valuable instrument of learning.

CONTENTS

THE WHY OF THE ROCKS

Why we think of the Alps as young mountains

During the many millions of years of its history the Earth's crust suffered countless upheavals. They resulted in the formation of innumerable chains of mountains.

No trace whatever now remains of the oldest of these because they were completely eroded away by atmospheric forces. Some remnants of others still persist but they are buried beneath strata, or layers, of more recent rocks. At the present time the highest peaks are the newest ones; they are high just because water and other influences were too late to level them completely.

The Alps, the Himalayas and the Rocky Mountains began to rise about 65 million years ago; they are, therefore, quite old, but to the geologist they are still young because the unit of measurement which he uses to record such enormous natural events is equal to millions of years.

According to modern discoveries the Alps are still rising slowly but the amount which they gain in height is continually cancelled out by erosion.

The chief cause of their upheavals is to be found in the thrust exerted by the African continent. It moved northwards and forced the rock strata of the Mediterranean Basin to pile up against the lands of Europe which had emerged earlier, and to form the present parallel chains of mountains.

The Alps consist of numerous ranges divided by deep valleys. They stretch from the Gulf of Genoa to Vienna and rise between the plains of northern Italy and of southern Germany.

This diagram of the hill above consists of a sheet of basalt, decomposed at its base, resting on layers of sand and gravel

Why mountains die

To anyone who visits the mountains and sees them the same and unmoving year after year, this may appear impossible. Nevertheless day by day the mountains are being eaten away and changed. The erosive action of wind, rain and frost wears them away, little by little, removing from their walls rock particles, which are ceaselessly carried downwards.

The speed of erosion varies with the hardness of the rocks and the intensity of the rain, wind and storms which pound against the face of the rocks. However all mountains finish by being worn away and disintegrating until they are levelled out. Of course this takes hundreds of millions of years to happen. During this time the life of a mountain can be divided into three parts: youth, maturity and old age.

Why some mountains have perpendicular walls

Let us imagine that a huge area of the Earth's crust gradually rises above the surface of the seas and keeps its horizontal position.

When a certain point is reached, an enormous vertical or inclined crack, miles and miles long, appears in this mass of super-elevated rocks and part of the mass begins to sink whilst the remainder stays still or continues to rise.

Eventually there will be a great difference in height between the two masses. This will expose the strata of the rocks which remain upright so as to form very imposing mountains with perpendicular walls.

A view of part of the coast of the Isle of Wight

Why some rocks are known as sandstone rocks

As the name implies sandstone rocks are formed of grains of sand cemented together. They contain a very high proportion of quartz or silica material, but the composition varies a good deal according to the area where the alluvial sand deposits were stratified.

However, sandstone rocks are subdivided more on the basis of the binding materials which hold them together than the composition of the grains.

In this way we have sandstone rocks with calcareous cement, in which the grains of quartz and other rocks are bonded in very fine particles of calcite; sandstone with argillaceous cement, very hard and compact; sandstone with ferruginous cement, and so on.

Some very beautiful sandstones are the ones with mica cement, in which the flakes of mica are arranged in parallel planes, giving characteristic streaks to the stone.

Because of their mainly alluvial origin, sandstone rocks are widely distributed on the Earth's surface and can be very old indeed.

Others, however, are very recent and show only the beginnings of cementing.

In addition to being used as building material, sandstone is also used to make grindstones. As it is porous sandstone formations are valuable storage basins and sources of water.

Why there is such a great variety of rocks

The first rocks which were formed by the Earth's crust were all the same. They were the result of the cooling down and solidifying of white-hot magma, or molten rock. In the course of many millions of years various atmospheric forces gradually caused these rocks to disintegrate, splitting them into smaller and smaller pieces.

The products of this breaking down process were carried down by streams and deposited in layers, which got higher and higher. These rock materials, bonded together and changed in various ways by many chemical and mechanical agents, are the sedimentary rocks. They are different in appearance not only because of their age and the materials from which they came, but also because of the effect of being deposited and transformed chemically by other substances added to them in the course of millions of years. The oldest of the sedimentary rocks are buried at the bottom with newer and more recent rocks piled above them.

12

Why some rocks are much sought after

All the rocks found in nature are formed by the combination of one or more simple minerals bonded together. If we wish to isolate and obtain in the pure state the various minerals of which these rocks are composed, we usually have to submit them to special processes. The technique of these changes from time to time and can be more or less complex.

One of the easiest, and therefore one which man has used since the beginning of civilization, for obtaining minerals such as copper, lead and iron is by heating the rocks which contain them up to a very high temperature, the fusion temperature.

On the other hand, the process by which aluminium is obtained is a rather complicated one. Although it exists in very large amounts in the rocks of the Earth's crust, this metal was first isolated in sufficient quantities only at the beginning of the last century. In order to obtain it the aluminium bearing minerals have

to be subjected to a process of electrolysis.

Nowadays the technique of extracting useful minerals and metals from the rocks has reached a very high degree of specialization.

Some substances, which are rare in nature but of great value in industry, such as titanium, uranium and thorium, are extracted from the minerals which contain them even though the operation is very difficult and expensive.

To obtain the rocks containing them we explore forests and deserts and scale mountains, building roads and railways and even complete towns to make possible the digging and transportation of these metals to the processing plant.

Rocks containing rare minerals are very valuable and their deposits are very much sought after.

Why basalt rocks are rust-coloured

Basalt, a volcanic rock which is quite common, is very easy to recognize by its colour, ranging from black to dark green, its compactness and its heavy weight. However basalt rocks which have been exposed to the air over a long period become covered on the surface with a reddish coating, very similar to rust. This happens because this rock usually contains various iron compounds which become oxidized by the action of the atmosphere.

Where there are very large and compact deposits of basalt these rocks can be found in the form of columns or pillars. The lava issuing white hot from the bowels of the Earth cools on the surface and forms structures of hexagonal or six-sided columns joined tightly to one another and arranged perpendicular to the surface.

Why some rocks split into sheets

All metamorphic rocks, that is those which have undergone great changes, which have a lamellar or fibrous structure and can therefore be divided into sheets, sometimes very thin sheets, are called schists. This structure is caused by the crushing and parallel arrangement of the components of the primitive rock.

Some very common schists are mica, chlorites and talc which, because of their plate-like formation, can be split along parallel lines.

After being formed schists may undergo other changes by contraction, high pressure or variations of temperature. We then have what are known as crystalline schists.

A great variety of these are found and are named according to the elements of which they are composed. For instance, we have mica schists formed mostly of quartz and mica; quartzites; calcareous schists containing calcite; phyllite composed of quartz and mica in very fine laminations; talc schists, and many others.

Why primitive man used flint tools

Flint is fairly common in rocks of all ages. It contains a high proportion of silicate of a special crystalline structure, making it both hard and fragile at the same time.

Primitive man usually found it along the river banks in the form of large pebbles. By striking them in a particular way he broke them into sharp flakes.

These pieces of flint were very useful for scraping, cutting, sawing and polishing. Fixed on the end of a stick, they could inflict serious wounds on the large animals which man hunted.

Until metals came on the scene much later, flint was the inseparable companion of early man because its fine grain and brittleness made it better than any other stone for forming the implements and tools which he needed.

Many different kinds of flint tools were made and innumerable examples of them have been found. It is sometimes possible to trace ancient trade routes by knowing where a particular type of flint was obtained.

Why some rocks split into slabs

As opposed to crystalline shale, argillaceous or clayey shale is of a very fine grain structure.

The schistosity of these rocks is perfect and they can be split into very large sheets and very thin sheets. They are to be found in many parts of the country and have been used for centuries for covering and roofing houses. The most valuable of them, called slate, is still employed for making the large blackboards used in schools.

Sometimes because of the high proportion of mica flakes, the sheets of these clayey shales have a very bright appearance. They frequently contain fossils which are nearly always imperfect and in a poor state of preservation. This is as a result of the same phenomena of pressure and crushing which changed the sedimentary into metamorphic rocks.

15

Why the diamond is a precious stone

Generally speaking precious stones are no more than fragments of minerals which have crystallized in a different way from normal. They owe their value not so much to the costliness of their materials as to their rarity.

There are many types of gem but only four really deserve the title of 'precious': the diamond, the emerald, the sapphire and the ruby. The diamond has been known for at least 3,000 years and is the hardest mineral found in nature. This quality, together with those of beauty and rarity, make it the most precious stone in the world.

In its natural state this precious stone is certainly not one of the most magnificent. On his sixty-sixth birthday King Edward VII was presented with the largest diamond in the world (it weighed 3,106 carats) which was found in the Transvaal in 1905. When he saw the rough appearance and lack of lustre of the stone, he is reported to have said: 'If I had seen it in the street, I would have kicked it away like an ordinary piece of glass.'

A little later this famous 'piece of glass' was cut with the greatest skill by Asscher's in Amsterdam into nine major gems and ninety-six small brilliants. The biggest gem, known as the Great Star of Africa, is the largest cut diamond in the world. That and the second largest gem are part of the British crown jewels and are on display in the Tower of London.

Why some stones were made into amulets and seals

The beautiful rare coloured stones, often of small size, which are found in caves or in the beds of rivers, attracted men's attention from the very earliest times. Our ancestors could not explain where these small sparkling stones came from. The very bright colours were quite unlike any rocks with which they were acquainted.

Being superstitious, they thought they were signs from the gods and that to possess such stones gave them divine protection against all kinds of misfortune. That is why amulets were made and we know from archeological discoveries that they were used in prehistoric times.

In the course of time and with the progress of civilization men began to make these precious stones even more beautiful and sparkling by polishing them, cutting them into regular shapes and mounting them in holders of precious metals such as gold and silver. Someone also had the idea of cutting into them decorative and personal designs, so that the owner could recognize them easily if they were mislaid or stolen.

When stones prepared in this way were pressed on to a tablet of soft clay they left in it the impression of the design. That is how the first seals came into being, and they were used on clay tablets in Babylon some 5,000 years ago. Some of these seals were in the form of cylinders.

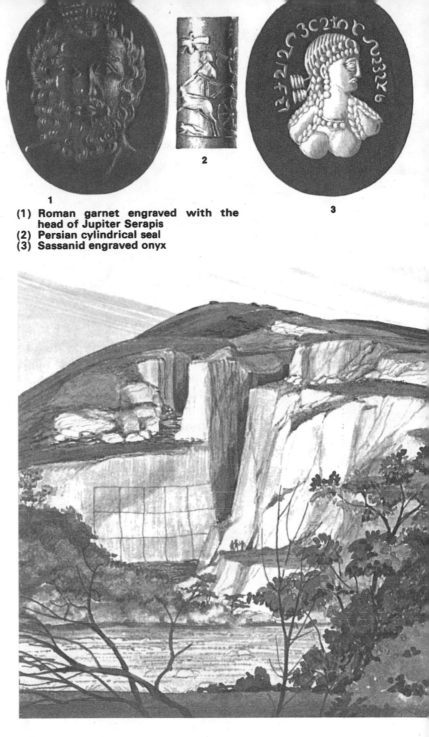

(1) **Roman garnet engraved with the head of Jupiter Serapis**
(2) **Persian cylindrical seal**
(3) **Sassanid engraved onyx**

Why some mountains are made of marble

From the geological point of view marble is a calcareous or limestone rock of crystalline structure. Limestone is a sedimentary rock usually formed beneath the seas by the depositing of enormous layers of shells of small sea animals. But normal limestone is not marble. It can be turned into marble in various ways.

For instance, if the limestone layers are covered by lava, the heat of the molten mass changes the surrounding rock by fusion into crystallized limestone, that is true marble. Sometimes crystallization is the result of very high pressure.

Even the purest marbles contain other minerals such as quartz, colouress or pale yellow mica and dark flakes of graphite.

17

Why there are volcanoes

Thousands of millions of years ago the Earth was a burning sphere. Gradually it cooled down and in the course of time its rocky crust solidified. We now know, because of a theory called Plate Tectonics, that the earth's crust is made up of raft-like plates which are slowly moving. The areas between the plates are unstable and subject to volcanic activity. Most volcanoes occur when two plates collide. One rides up over the other which sinks and remelts creating an underground reservoir of lava. Some of the melted rock rises to the earth's crust and, due to the pressure between the two plates erupts in the form of a volcanoe.

Inflammable vapours may break through a weak place in the surface rock, creating a volcano

If a large gap occurs between the two plates, the compressed matter may escape through it. When this happens there is what we call a volcanic eruption. Lava and other matter gush out from the inside of the Earth where the molten rock is still white hot.

Why lava is not always the same

Depending on its composition and temperature the lava flowing out of a volcano can be either liquid or viscous (sticky). The first generally comes from the crater at a temperature of about 1,100°C and contains a great deal of iron, magnesium and calcium. The second, on the other hand, is at a lower temperature and contains high percentages of silica and alumina.

The fluid lava, of course, forms the fastest deposits. They are the ones, therefore, which can very quickly reach the lower slopes of the volcano and cause a great deal of destruction.

Once the eruption is over, the surface of the lava hardens very quickly to form a rocky crust, although it still remains fluid underneath.

If the side of the volcano is steep, it can happen that the underlying lava continues to descend whilst the crust remains motionless. In this way the so-called vacuum spaces or lava tunnels are formed.

Soil of lava origin is very fertile and, therefore, despite the danger, human settlements are always to be found in volcanic regions.

Why there are earthquakes

If we try to record on a map those places in the world where earthquakes most frequently happen, we find that they coincide to a very surprising degree with the volcanic zones of the Earth's surface

The explanation of this is quite simple. Earthquakes are rapid and violent vibrations of the Earth's crust as from time to time, in the most unstable places, it settles down into new positions.

Since the unstable zones are precisely those where the fissures occur which give rise to the volcanic outlets, it is clear that where there are volcanoes there is also the risk of earthquakes.

In fact some earthquakes are linked directly with volcanic activity. That is to say that they are caused either by internal explosions of steam or by the upward pressure of volcanic materials trying to break through the Earth's crust.

There are also earthquakes which are due to the settling down of the crust of the Earth and these are not connected with volcanoes.

San Francisco

Why water is the enemy of the rocks

If we follow a stream or river from its source to its mouth we can see that from the very beginning it is a great enemy of the rocks and soil.

Whether it comes from a glacier or a spring or merely from flood waters, it attacks the soil right away and carries down with it sand and pieces of rock, which twist and bump here and there like hammers, breaking up the river banks.

This erosive action is particularly strong in mountainous areas where the water flows down steep slopes. Even in the plains where it moves more slowly, however, the river continues to break off and carry away the soil, widening its bed and making twists and turns, particularly during floods.

Why treeless mountains are more exposed to erosion

If heavy rains fall on to a mountain forest only some of the water runs away at once. The brushwood and vegetation retain more than half of it in small pools or merely in scattered drops.

But if the rain falls on a bare mountain, streams and torrents are formed immediately and flow impetuously down the slopes, gouging out tiny valleys and carrying away large amounts of soil.

In this case fast flowing water is one of the most active agents of rock destruction. The work of erosion differs, of course, from one type of soil to another.

In argillaceous, or clay, mountains such as the Appenines in Italy, for example, the water scoops

out characteristic gullies formed of numerous minute valleys separated by dividing walls.

In granite areas the rain loosens and carries away all the oxidized and decomposed rock particles, and creates a landscape of rounded masses of rock.

Finally in mixed areas, pyramids of rock can be formed. The surrounding ground is removed from around the heavier masses which then act as a shade for the earth beneath.

This phenomenon is the cause of the rocky ridges surmounted by huge boulders which are typical of certain scenes in the American West, in the arid zones of the Rocky Mountains.

Why we are sure that the Earth was once covered by enormous glaciers

The surest sign that a glacier reached a certain place is the presence of moraines.

These are always composed of deposits of rocks, loam and mud which a glacier carries with it during its slow movement and which accumulate at the points where the tongues of ice melt. These moraines tell us that over a million years ago in the Pleistocene Period there was a considerable fall in the temperature on Earth. The cold became more and more intense, and immense sheets of ice advanced from Siberia and Greenland and invaded Europe, Asia and North America.

It was like a very long winter which lasted for about 100,000 years, during which there was continuous snow. As the snow collected in enormous layers on the continents, the seas and oceans,

which were no longer being fed by the rivers, began to fall in level. Water continued to evaporate and form clouds but it was not replaced by the rain water which normally returns to the seas.

Some of the glaciers which exist today are left over from the Pleistocene Period when ice covered three times as much of the Earth's surface as it does at present.

Before the Pleistocene Ice Age there were two earlier periods when ice covered areas which are now tropical. The first occurred about 600 million years ago in Pre-Cambrian times, and the other was during the Permian Period, some 235 million years ago.

21

Why some soils are rich in water and others not

The subsoil is composed of rock strata which differs from one region to another. Under the surface layer of soil there can be layers of gravel, clay or solid rock which vary in the extent to which they allow water to pass through them.

With the same rainfall a soil can be fertile or not according to

its capacity to retain the water which it receives from the skies. If it is not very porous the water remains on the surface and evaporates in a short time, whereas if the rain penetrates deeply, the moisture is retained in the soil much longer and provides ideal conditions for plant growth.

However, it may happen that the rain water meets no obstacle

after the first layer of soil and continues to sink below the level of the roots. This means that beneath the layer of soil there is another layer which acts as a sponge or a layer of calcareous rock, letting the water through. By hidden ways the water then travels through the subsoil until it is caught and channelled by an impervious layer of rock which forces the water to follow its slope.

The porous soil on the surface then becomes arid and dry, whilst the soil where there are strata of impervious rocks is rich in springs; in fact the water is stopped in its subterranean journey and turned by these rocks towards the surface again.

It can also happen that the layers of impervious rocks over which the water runs in the subsoil are at a lower level than the surrounding plains or even below sea level. Pockets of water are then formed far below the surface and in this case the water can be recovered from deep wells.

Why caves are formed in limestone rocks

Limestone areas often have caves and underground crevices as a result of water action. They contain the largest caves and the greatest number of caves of the Earth's surface. Some can only be entered in dry weather as they are completely filled with water during the rainy seasons.

To understand how the water can have dug out the rock in this way we have to remember that limestone dissolves in water containing carbon dioxide, and that there are often deep natural fissures due to the settling down of the Earth's crust.

As the rain falls through the atmosphere it takes up carbon dioxide from the air in small amounts and therefore becomes a solvent for this type of rock. Running along the surface or falling into the natural crevices the water dissolves the surface of the limestone and carries it away.

In the course of time these crevices become wider and longer and are transformed into wells. Underground the water tries to find a way out through the cracks and the rock layers.

In this way we get underground rivers which by their continued work of erosion over hundreds of thousands of years scoop out large deep caves.

Sometimes this erosion is accompanied by landslides and falls which change the land greatly and form depressions known as sink-holes.

Why sink-holes are always round

One of the most characteristic of these mountain areas is the Carso, a limestone area along the Dalmatian coast which is strangely and irregularly covered with large and roundish holes. In some parts if there were no houses or streets it would seem like a Moon landscape full of craters. This kind of landscape is also found in the Pennines in England and in the French Causses. It occurs in many places in America and in the tropics.

Although these sink-holes look like craters, they are in no way due to volcanic action. In fact, they are caused by the slow but persistent wearing action of rain water.

The surprising thing about these

The beautiful features of a cave in a limestone area

sink-holes is that they are always round; this is due to the rotary movement of the water, which acts on the rock like the point of a giant drill. Sometimes if the limestone layer is thick, the work of excavation is continued underground and forms wells and deep pits thousands of metres deep.

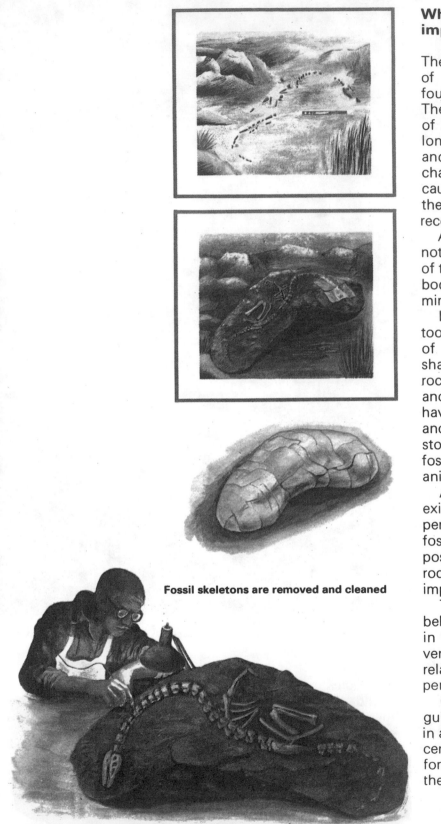

Fossil skeletons are removed and cleaned

Why fossils in rocks are important

The rocks in which fossil remains of animals and plants can be found are the sedimentary rocks. These were made from the deposits of mud and sand which in ages long past filled the depressions and seas, forming layers and changing into compact rocks. Because of the fossils embedded in them, sedimentary rocks contain a record of life since the earliest times.

Animals buried in this mud did not decompose quickly because of the special conditions and their bodies became saturated with mineral salts.

In the course of time these salts took the place of the organic cells of the body and retained their shape. Now when we break the rocks, we find the bodies of ancient living creatures which have kept their original appearance but have been turned into stone. This is what happened to fossil shells and many other marine animals.

All these animals (and plants) existed during a well defined period of time. When we find fossils in a layer of rock, it is possible to discover the age of the rock by the types of animals imprisoned in it.

There are some fossils which belong to animals which lived in every part of the world in very large numbers but only during relatively short and well defined periods.

Geologists call them 'fossil-guides' because their presence in an area indicates with complete certainty that those rocks were formed during a certain period of the Earth's history.

Why there is little coal in some countries

Coal is formed from the remains of trees, plants and shrubs which grew many millions of years ago. Its quality depends on the nature of the original plants as well as on the subsequent effects of pressure, temperature and time.

In Britain coal has developed from the dense forests which existed over 300 million years ago in the Carboniferous Period. Although poor in mineral resources Britain produces about 5 per cent of the world coal output.

In some parts of the world, however, coal seams are very poor, but conditions have been favourable for the formation of lignite and peats, which are more recent coals. Between lands which rose gradually from the sea large lake beds were formed which then became deposits of lignite. This type of coal which is not yet completely formed, shows in many cases quite clear indications of wood structure. It breaks easily and is powdery, and before it is sold it has to be compressed into bricks.

About 21 million tons of lignite are mined annually in the United States and lignite resources are a major factor in the development of eastern and south-eastern Europe.

An even more recent formation is peat, which is formed of marsh plants which have been carbonized and still continue to change beneath the mud of marshy ground.

Peat is brown in colour, has an earthy and fibrous appearance and contains a good deal of moisture. It, too, has to be dried or compressed into bricks before use.

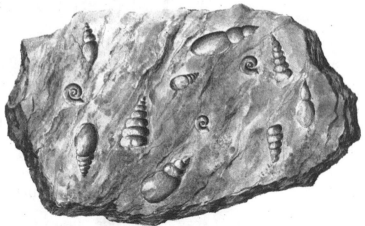

Fossiliferous limestone

Why there are sea shells in the mountains

Have you ever wondered how fossils of sea shells became embedded in mountain rocks?

A little experiment will give you the answer. In a flat bottomed dish containing about 5 centimetres of water place a large, fairly stiff cloth. With one hand keep one end of the cloth firm on the bottom while with the other hand you slowly push the opposite end of the cloth towards the fixed end. Under the thrust the cloth will fold and finally rise until it reaches the surface of the water.

Millions of years ago the same thing happened at the bottom of the oceans. The cloth represents the numerous strata of sand and mud containing shells which had been deposited over a long period of time in the bottom of the sea, solidifying and becoming compact rocks. In nature the pressure of the hand is replaced by enormous forces which in certain circumstances pressed on the strata folding and raising them.

THE WHY OF PLANTS AND ANIMALS

Why fungi are not green like other plants

For their food most plants make use of a special substance by means of which water and mineral salts (absorbed from the soil) and carbon dioxide (absorbed from the air) are changed into the starches which are necessary for growth. This substance, which is what gives plants their green colour, is called chlorophyll and the process of transformation is called photosynthesis because it needs the light of the Sun.

There are, however, some plants which do not have any chlorophyll and are therefore able to grow in the dark. Fungi, for example, can be grown even in caves, and truffles actually grow underground. These plants, lacking any chlorophyll, are therefore not green, and need organic substances produced by other plants. That is why fungi live on the trunks and roots of dead trees.

Why the coconut palm is called the king of the vegetable kingdom

The coconut palm grows along the coasts of Africa and in other tropical areas. Some people call it the king of plants because of the wide range of products which can be obtained from it.

It is a beautiful tree with a strong trunk growing to a height of nearly 33 metres and ending in a tuft of fan-shaped leaves, each of them from 4 to 5 metres in length. Male and female flowers develop in the axils of the leaves and are in small inflorescences or groups.

The fruit which they produce are well known oval coconuts weighing as much as 2 kilos. When they are on the trees, however, the nuts are not the dark brown colour which we know. They are covered with a thick fibrous husk, green in colour, which is removed before the coconut is put on sale. The fibres are used for making matting and ropes.

A palm tree can produce as many as ten bunches of coconuts, each composed of ten to twelve nuts. Beneath the brown woody shell, which is sometimes used for making buttons, we find the coconut 'seed', that is the white pulp, rich in sugar, fats and protein which we love to eat. A drink called toddy is also produced from the sap of the young stalks.

Morel *(Morchella esculenta)*

Sarsosoma globosum

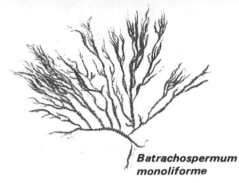

Batrachospermum monoliforme

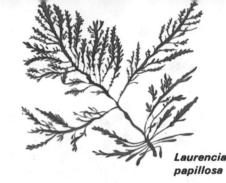

Laurencia papillosa

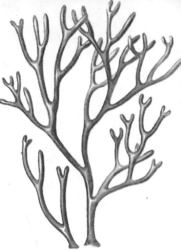

Codium tomentosum

Why seaweed is found in so many different colours

There are many kinds of seaweed living in the sea and you can often find pieces of them on the beach where they have been·left by the tide.

The commonest are the green ones which are found in the shallowest parts of the sea and which almost reach the surface. The brown and red varieties of seaweed grow at deeper levels.

It has recently been shown that there is a very good reason behind the distribution of the various types of seaweed in the sea bed. The coloured pigments which distinguish them from one another serve, in fact, to enable them to use the light of the Sun, which becomes weaker as the water gets deeper.

For instance, the red rays are filtered first by the sea water and are therefore stopped at a shallow depth. These rays are practically the only ones used by the green seaweeds which are therefore on the sea bed nearest to the surface.

The brown ones and in particular the red ones, on the other hand, can live below a depth of 100 metres because they are also able to make use of the green rays of the sunlight which can penetrate to such depths.

Each ocean has its own distinct varieties of seaweed and a large percentage of the species in any one ocean is not found elsewhere.

Why willow trees are so common in the country

There are almost 500 species of willow scattered over a large area from the tropics to the northern zones. To the *Salix* or willow family belongs the tiniest tree we know. It is the dwarf willow which is only a few centimetres high and grows in the mountains right up on the snow line.

Willow trees are found everywhere in the country because men have used them for all kinds of purposes since the earliest times. For thousands of years, in fact, these trees with their very pliable branches have supplied the raw materials for weaving baskets and for making furniture.

Corallina officinalis

Deiesseria sanguinea

Why trees change colour in autumn

Every year with the approach of autumn the trees come to their period of rest. Little by little the leaves turn yellow and then curl up and fall to the ground. The tree then remains almost completely inactive until the return of good weather in the spring. It is a sad sight but at the same time a wonderful one, because before dropping the leaves turn to shades of yellow, brown and red.

The explanation of this is quite simple. Plants are living organisms and must have food, and this they obtain by utilizing the organic substances provided by the leaves. At the same time, like animals, they also produce waste matter.

Animals are able to get rid of the waste materials from their food but the plant has to retain them in its tissues until the autumn. When the time comes for the leaves to fall, the plant extracts from them all the products which can be used, leaving behind the waste materials. This is what gives the foliage its yellow, brown and red colours.

Why trees lose their leaves in autumn

In autumn the leaves of many trees change colour and then gradually fall and the branches become bare.

Other trees like the pine, the fir, the laurel and the holly keep their green foliage even in the winter, and you may therefore think that they do not need to change their leaves every year.

This is not so; even the evergreen plants change their old leaves for new ones, but they do it a little at a time throughout the whole year. This can be seen from the layer of dry needles which are to be found under fir trees.

All plants change their leaves, but why?

There are many reasons. In the case of broad-leaved plants there is the problem of defence against the cold. If they kept their foliage during the winter they would expose an enormous area to the frost, equal to that of all the leaves put together side by side.

In addition the plant needs rest and therefore discards all those tiny chemical workshops which evaporate water in large amounts and call on the roots to supply more and more.

But the main reason for the change, even for the evergreens, is that eventually the chemical laboratories in the leaves get old and need to be replaced by new and efficient ones. The shorter days of autumn hastens this change.

When the old leaf has fallen, a healing layer forms on the stem and closes the wound, leaving the leaf scar. This can be seen clearly on many twigs in winter and is one of the marks by which trees are identified.

Why clover makes the land fertile

Clover is easily distinguished from the other grasses of the meadows.

It is a very important plant not only because it is widely cultivated for animal food but also because wherever clover grows the soil becomes more fertile after a certain time.

The roots of this tiny plant have small nodules containing special bacteria which are able to absorb nitrogen from the air and fix it in the earth.

Since nitrogenized substances are among those mostly used by plants, land which has had the benefit of the activity of clover roots becomes much more suitable for cultivation.

Why the fig is not a real fruit

The part of the fig tree which we call the fruit is, in fact, a very fleshy flower closed in on itself like a small bag. Numerous minute flowers with very simple petals open on the inside and can be seen when the unripe fig is opened. Each one of these flowers actually produces a small dry fruit; these are the tiny seeds which we find when we eat the sugary pulp of the fig.

Fig trees are typically Mediterranean plants. They often grow wild and are used to form hedges along the roads and to cover rocky and steep slopes.

The fig is so widely used in Mediterranean countries that it is called 'the poor man's food'. When they are ripe the leaves are gathered and are stored or sold for cattle fodder.

Why leaves exposed to the Sun do not get hot

If during the warmest part of the summer we put sheets of paper or fragments of any material in the Sun, we find after some time that they are very hot. If they are metal they may well become hot enough to burn us.

On the other hand, the leaves on trees are exposed all day long to the Sun but when we touch them they are always fresh as if the Sun's rays had not fallen on them.

Their continued freshness is due to the fact that they evaporate ceaselessly an incredible amount of water, the residue of the complicated chemical changes which take place inside them.

This evaporation causes a fall of temperature so that they always feel cool to the touch.

Why the leaves of the *Victoria regia* float on the water

The *Victoria regia* which can be admired in the tropical houses of many European botanical gardens, grows in the natural state in the dense forests of the Amazon region. It is a typical aquatic plant related to the water-lily.

The peculiar thing about it is the enormous development of the leaves. They are like great circular vessels with raised edges and can grow to a size of more than 2 metres in diameter.

These leaves float on the water and there is no risk of their sinking. The largest ones can even support the weight of a child without becoming submerged.

This ability to float is due to the fact that the leaf tissues contain innumerable tiny air pockets which make the leaves light in weight and create the same conditions as those which enable even very heavy ships to float.

Why the banana is a plant and not a tree

The large bunches of bananas which we see on sale in the shops come from a plant similar to a palm, from 3 to 10 metres in height. It is not really a tree but a giant plant which grows vigorously from an underground stem or rhizome which dies after producing its fruit.

What seems like a trunk is in fact made of the superimposed sheaths of the large leaves which form a bunch of foliage like palm trees. The leaves are very fragile and the wind frays the edges.

The fruit is at first a flowery growth on the top of the plant but after pollination the female flowers develop into bananas, which scientifically are regarded as berries without any seeds. Between fifty and 150 bananas, grouped in clusters, grow on each plant.

That the banana is a plant and not a tree is also shown by the fact that each stalk only lives for one year. As soon as the fruit has come to full maturity the plant dries up and dies. In the meantime, however, the rhizome puts out fresh shoots and thus ensures the growth of new plants.

Why there are so many different varieties of pumpkin

Pumpkins have been the subject of extensive cultivation and constant crossing which has produced thousands of varieties, with giant fruit and small fruit and of varying shapes and colours.

The pumpkin plant is a very strange vegetable. It has a hard, woody stem and bears the largest and heaviest fruit known. Certain pumpkins attain a weight of as much as 50 kilos although the usual weight is between 5 and 10 kilos.

Moreover, it is one of the fastest growing plants. Starting from a tiny seed, in about four months it grows a stem as long as 40 metres. The stem is completely hollow and has enormous water vessels which are visible to the naked eye. Very large amounts of water are evaporated from its leaves.

Pumpkins are grown in North America, Great Britain and Europe.

They are used as a vegetable, in puddings and pies and also for animal feed.

Why nettles sting when you touch them

Everyone knows the nettle if only because of the unpleasant burning sensation it causes on the skin when touched.

The leaves and stems of the nettle are covered with hairs in the shape of tiny tubes which burst at the slightest touch and sprinkle an irritating fluid on to the skin.

It seems, however, that this liquid does not have any effect on ducks because these birds love to eat nettle leaves.

Nettles are also difficult weeds because, like couch grass, they produce runners.

The point about them is that they are much weaker than the stems above ground and therefore when you pull up a nettle, part of the root breaks off and remains in the ground. More nettles shoot up from the pieces left behind.

Why couch grass is such a nuisance

Couch grass, which is also called quack grass or quitch grass, is a very common weed. It is found in gardens and cultivated fields and is often the despair of gardeners because it even creeps into flower beds and is very difficult to get rid of.

It is in fact a weed which has a very special way of reproducing itself. The plant pushes out a number of underground shoots known as runners. These put down roots at regular intervals and give rise to new plants.

If you pull out a handful of couch grass the ivory coloured runners break and leave part behind in the ground and after a while new plants spring up from them.

Urtica dioica (right)—Nettle.

Cross-section of poison gland (left and centre)

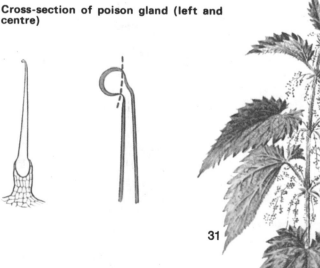

31

A cassowary

Why the cassowary kicks the plants it feeds on

Because of this strange habit the cassowary is regarded as having a very bad temper.

It can often be seen giving furious kicks at the trunks of trees without any apparent reason.

In fact the cassowary is thought to be a timid bird but if we remember that it has very strong legs and that it feeds mainly on fruit, we can see the reason for those blows; they are to shake the plant and make the fruit and ripe berries fall to the ground.

The cassowary lives in New Guinea and the nearby islands and one species reaches the north-eastern tip of Australia. With the emu and the ostrich it is one of the largest living birds, growing to a height of more than one and a half metres. It is unable to fly but is a very fast runner and can reach speeds of up to 50 kilometres an hour. On each foot it has three toes, the inner one having a long, straight, stiletto-like claw.

Cassowaries live in family groups or in pairs in tropical and mid-mountain forests. They like to be near water, for they swim readily and are good fishers.

Why some birds have very long legs

Birds with such legs are usually aquatic birds. The long legs enable them to move about in the shallow water of marshes, searching for the small fish and shellfish on which they live.

The plumage of some of these birds, in particular the herons and egrets, is really magnificent. To make it even finer two tufts of feathers stand up from the head like decorative ribbons.

In the egret, which is smaller than the heron, the plumage is completely white. These birds which live in marshy places are nevertheless pursued by hunters who use all kinds of tricks to capture them.

Against their guns the egrets

A heron

can only offer their swift, high flight, but against the hunters' dogs they do not hesitate to use their strong beaks and peck at the dogs' eyes with well aimed blows.

At one time ornithologists, that is scientists who make a study of birds, put all long-legged birds into one class and called them wading birds, but now they think that this classification is too broad.

These birds are now generally divided into three classes: the herons with long beaks and very slender and flexible necks; the cranes which are of various sizes but are all excellent walkers; and the last category comprising many species, mostly marine.

Why some caterpillars move in a long line

The commonest caterpillar in Italy and the one which has perhaps the most feared chemical defence is the processionary caterpillar of the pine woods, which has very irritating hairs.

If you have been on holiday in Italy and walked into a pine wood you may have seen strange processions of caterpillars of a greyish brown colour coming down from the trees and continuing along the ground, always following a precise line of march. There are hundreds of them in close touch with one another, following the leader who guides them in the search for food. Usually these journeys take place at night but these caterpillars are occasionally seen by day going up or down the rough bark of the pine trees.

The reason for this strange behaviour is that the processionary caterpillars are blind.

To find their feeding grounds they have to follow the leader who moves towards the leaves following his own instinct, and produces a fine silk thread which serves as a guide for the others, like the famous thread of Ariadne.

Why the kiwi has a very long beak

The kiwi's beak is long and thin because it is used for searching in the ground and under dead leaves for the caterpillars, worms and insects on which it feeds.

The kiwi hunts only at night

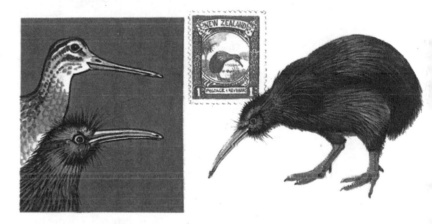

The kiwi, and (left) kiwi and snipe

and remains hidden during the daytime in thick bushes or in holes in the ground. Alone among birds the kiwi has a fine sense of smell. It is, perhaps, the last descendant of the large wingless bipeds which lived on the Earth in very remote times.

Kiwis mate for life. The female lays large eggs measuring about 7 by 12 centimetres, which are hatched by the male bird who sits on them for about eighty days.

The only living examples of these birds are to be found in the forests of New Zealand, where they are strictly protected to prevent their becoming extinct.

Why bats fly only at night

These small winged creatures have no need of sunlight. They swoop at night between houses and plants with surprising speed, catching the insects which they devour in large numbers. Every moment they have to avoid all kinds of obstacles but they are always able to do so by quick, deliberate movements.

A mysterious sixth sense guides them at night and enables them to 'see' the dangers and avoid them in time. This sixth sense works on a system something like our modern radar.

In fact, as it flies the bat emits a

series of very shrill sounds, so high pitched that our ears cannot pick them up. When some obstacle or object gets in its way these ultrasonic sounds are bounced off it and returned. All this takes place in a fraction of a second.

The bat hears, recognizes, calculates and veers away from the obstacle with a flap of the wings. It does this hundreds of times every night, for its brain is able to interpret complicated patterns of sound and echo with amazing speed.

Long before man was able to do so, therefore, this mammal learned to use the same principle on which radar is based.

But the bat's instrument is more perfect than ours.

The bat, in fact, is able to distinguish whether the object in its path is an obstacle or an insect, and can control its flight as required to avoid or approach.

Why the scorpion is said to eat with its legs

Before putting food into its mouth the scorpion minces it by rubbing it against its shell with its legs and pincers. This method of chewing outside the mouth is the remnant of a habit which was very common in ancient times when the first armoured creatures appeared. We know that the scorpion is a direct descendant of one of the first species of animal which populated the Earth.

From time immemorial these animals have captured the imagination of men by their monstrous shapes and very strange habits. A certain type of cannibalism is very common among scorpions: immediately after mating the female gobbles up the male.

Fruit bats at roost

34

Why the skunk never runs away

One of the animals which is really feared because of its terrible chemical weapon is the skunk, which lives in America. It is a omnivorous animal, eating both meat and plants, and is closely related to the weasel, ermine and polecat. Like them it has a soft fur.

But whereas the fur of the other animals of this group is of a colour which matches their surroundings, the typical skunk has a shaggy, glossy black coat marked by a white strip running from the back of the head to the tail. In fact this animal has no need to hide away in the woods to avoid meeting other animals. Quite the reverse, it is the others which sneak off as soon as he appears.

The skunk never runs away. When he is threatened he turns around swiftly, lifts up his bushy tail and launches at his enemy with incredible accuracy an evil smelling liquid produced by special glands.

This chemical defence is very

effective. The liquid is sprayed to a distance of several metres and has a really awful smell which it is difficult to get rid of even after repeated washing

Why the smallest European mammal is also one of the fiercest

The smallest mammal in Europe is the shrew, which can weigh as little as 2 grammes and be only a few centimetres long. Nevertheless, despite its extremely small size this animal is bloodthirsty and fierce and offers fight to any of its own species which it finds on its hunting ground.

It feeds mainly on insects, snails and worms and is said to eat almost continuously, consuming its own weight in food about every 3 hours. With the exception of snakes and some rapacious birds, the shrew has no enemies because no other animal dares to attack it.

Not only does it give off a nauseating smell from a gland on the side of its body when it is in danger, but it unleashes all its ferocity, becomes really enraged and does not hesitate to attack and bite anyone who tries to capture it, with no thought of escape.

It is not easy to find a shrew on the ground because of its small size, but if you should find one, do not try to pick it up in your hand or you will be bitten by this tiny, wild creature.

The short-tailed shrews, common to eastern North America, are reputed to have a poisonous bite; the toxin, however, is only powerful enough to affect the shrews' prey.

The tree shrews of southern Asia have bushy tails and look more like squirrels. They are dark olive brown in colour, with long, pointed muzzles. They feed on insects, some plants and the eggs and young of birds.

Etruscan shrew

35

Why the hippopotamus has protruding nostrils

Hippopotamuses live in herds near large African rivers and spend almost the whole day in the water, with only their eyes and nostrils showing. But the nostrils are very prominent on the nose so that the animals are able to breathe even when they are completely covered by water. In this way nature enables them to hide from their enemies.

Their food is exclusively vegetable, consisting of grass and marsh plants which the hippopotamus eats mainly at night when it comes out of the water.

Sometimes these animals become annoyed for no apparent reason and they will then lower their heads and attack even men. Normally, however, they are not dangerous.

The large African hippopotamus is more than 4 metres in length and weighs over 3 tons. In West Africa, however, there are some dwarf hippopotamuses which are only a quarter of the size of the large ones.

Hippopotamus

Why the fur of the polecat is not much sought after

The very name of this animal indicates the most characteristic feature for which it is known among hunters. It is a close relative of the marten and to protect itself it emits a nauseating smell produced by special glands.

The trouble is that the smell remains on the long, coarse fur of the animal even after being treated in all kinds of ways and for this reason the fur of the polecat is of little commercial value.

And yet the polecat is hunted fiercely because it is a bloodthirsty and ferocious animal feeding mostly on small mammals and any birds it can catch. It often makes its way into farms and slaughters poultry and rabbits. In winter it even takes up its abode close to the hen roosts and hides beneath piles of wood or in hollow trees.

If it did not have this wicked habit, the polecat could be regarded as an animal useful to farmers. Quick and agile, it destroys many rodents during its nocturnal excursions and does not hesitate to attack even vipers.

Why the rhinoceros likes to roll about in the mud

During the heat of the day the rhinoceros usually buries itself in muddy water, from which it emerges with a layer of mud on its skin. This dries and forms a protective coating against the bites of insects.

Despite the thickness of its hide, the rhinoceros is afraid of the bite of some parasites which inject it with germs of dangerous diseases. This fear seems very strange in such enormous animals, as much as 4 metres in length and covered with a thick hide like armour, but in the case of the rhinoceros it is another example of the fly beating the lion.

The legs of this beast are short and thick but this does not prevent it from running at a good speed, especially when charging an intruder who has annoyed it.

The African rhinoceros is common, particularly in the area of the great lakes of East Africa, because it prefers moist regions. Its habits are mostly nocturnal.

All species of rhinoceros are vegetarian: some browse on leaves and buds of shrubs and small trees, others graze on grasses.

Rhinoceroses are usually solitary, but a calf may accompany its mother for a long time, even after the birth of a younger offspring.

In former times, rhinoceroses inhabited both the eastern and western hemispheres, but now they live only in tropical Africa and Asia and are in danger of becoming extinct. The Asian rhinoceros has one horn, with the exception of the Sumatran which, like the African varieties, has two.

Rhinoceros

the *Platybelodon*, a mastodon as big as the present elephant, which walked along with its head down and its tusks thrust well into the ground, turning it over in search of the tubers, rhizomes and roots on which it fed.

In fact the name of this animal refers to the special shape of its lower jaw which, because it was used for 'ploughing' the ground was made like an enormous hollow shovel fitted at the sides with large flat incisors with cutting edges.

Why the elephant has long projecting tusks

Today the two enormous projecting teeth are of no use to the elephant, but if we could go back some 20 million years we would find an ancestor of this pachyderm which used its enormous tusks to turn over the earth in search of food. In those far-off days there were long stretches of plains deeply ploughed by long parallel grooves.

The author of these strange furrows in the grassy plains was

African elephant

Why the dromedary has a hump

The hump of the dromedary is nothing but a reserve of fat which the animal uses in case of need during long fasts in the desert. Indeed, after a tiring journey and a long time without food its hump looks flabby because it has been emptied of its food reserve.

The dromedary can actually cover a distance of as much as 170 kilometres in the desert with a load of 200 kilos. This will give you some idea of how useful this animal is: it has been employed since time immemorial for long and difficult journeys across the desert.

It cannot be said that the dromedary is an attractive animal. More stubborn than even a mule, it is rather stupid and bad tempered and can become dangerous if it is not treated properly. But in the desert it has no equal because nature has endowed it with very efficient means of surviving in those tremendous marches across the burning sands.

When the sandstorms blow in the desert, this animal crouches on the ground and tightly closes its eyes and nostrils. When there is no food and water it can go on for a long time by consuming the reserves in its hump and in internal sacs. It is, moreoever, very frugal and is content with simple vegetable food which it is able to find during the halts in its long marches.

Why crickets chirrup in the evening in the meadows

Everyone knows the cricket which breaks the silence of the summer evening with its incessant chirruping. The song of the cricket is a characteristic sound produced only by the males by rubbing one wing against the other. It seems certain that their nocturnal song is a love call to their female companions.

These crickets live beneath rocks and in small tunnels dug out of the earth, and they eat all kinds of food but prefer animal remains.

The black field cricket is one among about 2,000 species of cricket. Another well known variety is the house cricket, yellowish grey in colour, which hides away during the daytime and comes out at night in search of food. He, also, can produce the characteristic trill, and like his country cousin he is a very good jumper.

Why the dragon-fly is one of our oldest insects

When, walking near a stream or pond, we see the dragon-flies darting into the air, it is difficult to imagine that this advanced insect was one of the first to appear on Earth. And yet in the Carboniferous Period, over 260 million years ago, dragon-flies were just as numerous as they are today among the vegetation of the marshes, but they were of enormous size.

In the Carboniferous basin of Commentry in France fossil remains have been found of a dragon-fly which has a wing span of 65 centimetres.

Why the koala bear does not live in our zoos

The eucalyptus trees of Australia are the usual home of the koala bear. He seems to have rather refined tastes because he feeds only on the aromatic leaves of four kinds of eucalyptus out of the 400 types which grow in Australia. He prefers those with a high oil content and eats about a kilo of leaves daily.

This is the real reason why the koala bear is never to be found in our zoos. If there are no fresh leaves of his 'special' eucalyptus trees, the small marsupial declines and dies.

There is one curious fact: in the soft fur of the koala bear you never find those annoying parasitic insects which persecute other animals. This is due directly to the koala bear's special type of food. The oils of the eucalyptus impregnate the fur and keep the parasites away.

Why the lizard always stays in the sunniest places

During the winter lizards disappear. Hidden away in holes among the rocks they fall asleep but at the first gentle rays of the Sun they wake up and go on to the rocks to bask in the sunshine, still moving slowly but already alert to everything that goes on around them.

They are very hungry after their long fast but food is scarce because not many insects have yet been awakened by the warmer weather.

They remain quite still for a long time, waiting for the Sun to give them back the energy they need for the hunt. If you try to approach a lizard cautiously, you will only distinguish it from the twigs and dry grass by looking carefully at the top of the sunny stones. Then you will see its body moving at regular intervals with its breathing. For the rest it is perfectly still.

But if you move even slightly or if there is the faintest noise to break the silence, this tiny reptile darts off at surprising speed, disappearing into a crevice or crack in the wall.

It will quickly come back again because the lizard is a cold-blooded animal and can not remain for long in the darkness of a hole.

It needs the Sun. That is why it is usually to be found on walls well exposed to the sunlight.

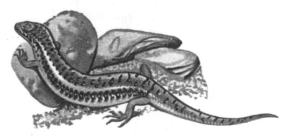

Why the bison is protected by special laws

When the great plains of North America were first colonized it is estimated that more than 60 million head of bison roamed freely over them. For the Indians these animals were the most important source of food and hides, but the redskins killed only the few head of bison required for their immediate needs and there was then no risk that the species might die out.

Then came the white man with his murderous firearms and began the mass slaughter of the bison. During the years when the great trans-continental railways were being built these poor animals were killed by the hundreds of thousands, for no good reason at all.

The colonists only used their tongues and other special parts and left the carcases to rot. Sometimes the animals were slaughtered just for sport. Bison bones were sold by the ton for a few dollars to the manufacturers of fertilizers.

It ended with the destruction of all the bison in the American territory except for a few head. These were saved and protected by special laws, and they are now beginning to increase in numbers once more.

The American bison, or buffalo as it is commonly called, is a large bovine animal with a massive head surmounted by two short curved horns. The male bison can weigh as much as a ton and reach a height of over 2 metres to the top of its large hump. Its coat is usually brown in colour with long hair around the head, neck and hump.

Why the slow-worm is not a true snake

If there is an innocent animal in the world which has suffered far too much and is still suffering for the wrongdoings of others it is the slow-worm. Perhaps you have seen one and thrown stones at it thinking it was a wicked snake, and all the time the poor slow-worm is not a snake at all even if it does look like one.

Moreover it is well known that this reptile loses its tail very easily, like a lizard. This happens because, in fact, the slow-worm is a lizard; a lizard which lost its legs a very long time ago and is therefore obliged to slide along the ground like a snake. It is quite harmless, however, so much so that it cannot even bite if you pick it up in your hand.

It has a very long body, greyish-brown and white in colour, with tiny bright scales. It is this which makes it look like a snake, but whereas snakes have glassy eyes without eyelids the slow-worm has eyelids which are easy to recognize and which are closed when it sleeps, making it appear blind. Perhaps that is why it got its name of slow-worm. This reptile prefers moist places and feeds on worms, grubs and snails.

Why the beaver builds dams

The ingenuity of the work done by a family of beavers arouses our astonishment and admiration. With its powerful, chisel-like incisors a beaver can cut down small shrubs at a single blow and in one or two nights' work can fell even quite large trees 30 centimetres in diameter. The beaver needs to be constantly gnawing because its incisor teeth continue to grow and if it did not wear them down against the wood of trees, it would have to keep its mouth permanently open and would die of a broken jaw.

The branches and trunks which it cuts down are used by the animal for its wonderful works of engineering.

The beaver builds comfortable, dome-shaped lodges for itself in the rivers, making them of stakes fixed in the mud and cemented with beaten earth. These lodges have two entrances, one below water and one above, and they are connected with runs on land. Water up to a certain level is essential in the lodge for the beaver's safety, and therefore in order to maintain the level this ingenious animal makes small artificial lakes by blocking the rivers with dams built of branches.

Until the last century beavers were very numerous in North America, particularly in the forests of Canada, but it has now become necessary to pass very strict laws to prevent this animal from being totally destroyed even there. Beaver fur was once very much in fashion and big trading companies sent bands of hunters to the North for the purpose of systematically hunting out all the beavers they could find.

Why the beavers' dams were thought to be dangerous

One of the reasons given by fur hunters to justify the massacre of beavers was that by their dams these animals could cause sudden floods. It is true that the water held back by the beavers' artificial barriers formed lakes of quite large size which during very heavy rains could rise to such an extent that the dams were carried away. The water would then flow back into the torrents and rivers, swelling them excessively and causing flooding over the banks.

It may be true that where the beavers' lakes have disappeared, the forests have become parched and dry.

Why the ladybird is useful to man

Beetles are among the most harmful insects both because of the number of species and also the greed of the larvae and of the adult individuals. However, in this very large family there is one which is the exception to the general rule, the charming ladybird with the seven spots and bright red wing-case which we all know.

Not more than half a centimetre long the ladybird is shaped like an egg which has been cut in half lengthwise and to which some inspired painter has given a coat of red enamel and then touched it up with a few decorative black spots.

It is very fond of aphides or greenfly which attack roses, and it is therefore a valuable ally of gardeners and farmers. Wherever there are ladybirds all the minute aphides which suck the lymph out of the plants disappear in a few days. The ladybirds kill them all off and devour them one by one. Even the eggs are deposited on plants infested with aphides so that when the tiny ladybirds hatch out they will feed on the greenfly. In one season several generations of ladybirds are born as their life cycle is only just over a month.

Sometimes when the cold weather comes these insects gather together in large numbers in sheltered places and spend the winter in hibernation. Although slow fliers they can migrate considerable distances. The ladybirds may be attacked and driven off by ants which regard greenfly as their own, extracting from them a sugary liquid, of which they are very fond.

Why some insects are divers

The water beetle, a beautiful beetle with a smooth bright shell, greenish brown in colour, which can live for a long time under water, is very common in ponds and stagnant water.

When it is immersed, the lower part of its body appears bright and silvery. This is due to a light layer of air which is held by the hair of the body and which enables the beetle to breathe even under water. When the air reserve is used up the water beetle comes to the surface to renew it.

However, this beetle does not spend all its time in the water. Often at dusk it flies around in the air attracted by the bright lights of nearby houses.

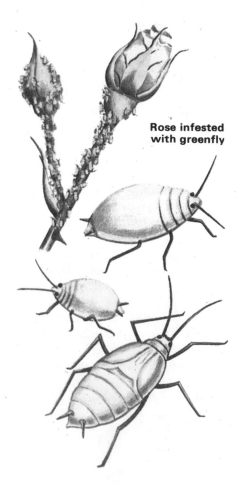

Rose infested with greenfly

Why the pond-skater is able to run on the water

In stagnant water and small calm pools, we can find the pond-skater, a tiny insect with long thin legs ending in fine hairs. Because of its light weight (the body is slender and only 2 centimetres in length) the pond-skater can walk swiftly on the surface of the water without sinking. In fact, the soft hairs of the legs take advantage of the fluid tension and just touch the surface ever so slightly and are held up by its elasticity.

It is as if the pond-skater were walking on a carpet of elastic.

Its name indicates how much running it does on the surface of ponds as if it wanted to measure the length and breadth of them. In reality, however, these movements are made for the sole purpose of searching for the tiny animals, living or dead, on which it feeds.

Another minute pond creature which possesses special acrobatic gifts is the water-boatman but its method of moving is just the opposite to that of the pond-skater. In fact the water-boatman walks below the level of the water, upside down, taking advantage of the surface tension.

On the surface of the water the water-boatman moves rather awkwardly with sudden leaps, but it prefers to stand for long periods, motionless, as if glued to a mirror, and from that position it lays in wait for small insects skimming along the water.

In Mexico this insect lays its eggs on bundles of straw which have been submerged in shallow water. These bundles are then collected and the eggs removed. They are used, mixed with cornmeal, in many Mexican dishes.

Why we find lots of snails after rain

After a shower of rain many snails come out among the grass and bushes. They can be seen moving slowly among the wet vegetation, carrying on their backs the shell, into which they are ready to retreat at the first sign of danger.

Snails need a great deal of moisture for their active life and that is why they come out after rain but retire into their shells and bury themselves in the ground during periods of drought.

In the winter they hibernate after sealing the opening of the shell with a plug of sticky material which keeps out the cold but allows air to pass through for breathing.

There are many kinds of snails, both land and water varieties, and some of them can be eaten.

The largest snails to be found in Europe have shells about 5 centimetres across but in Africa it is possible to discover examples of up to 20 centimetres long.

Slugs also need a great deal of moisture and they usually come out early in the morning when the dew is on the ground. They are very prolific and reproduce frequently and are real pests in the garden where their large numbers and greed cause very much damage.

Why snake charmers use the cobra

The cobra is one of the best known poisonous snakes.

It has become so widely known because of the snake charmers who are still to be found even today in the market places and fairs of southern Asia.

At the sound of a flute the cobra rises sinuously out of its wicker basket and appears to follow the modulations of the music by slow movements of its body.

Yet the cobra, like all snakes, does not hear sound transmitted through the air and cannot therefore be charmed by the music. It is, rather, the skill of the master who tamed it that mesmerizes the snake, causing it to sway rhythmically as if it were trying to dance.

Why the mole is almost blind

The mole is a small animal which is very common in the fields. Its whole body is perfectly designed for the underground life which it leads. Its nose is strong and pointed and acts like a wedge to penetrate the earth. The forefeet are shaped like shovels to dig out and move the soil. The body is round and flexible. The mole has no ear flaps which would be a nuisance in narrow tunnels.

As for eyes, what use are they in the darkness of the runs in which it lives? That is why they have become atrophied and reduced to two pin-heads hidden among the soft fur.

Nevertheless, it must be regarded as a useful animal because of its feeding habits. It lives almost entirely on the larvae of harmful insects which it finds by digging deep tunnels in the ground. It is a greedy animal, eating one- to two-thirds of its own weight daily. But to get at its food and dig its underground passages the mole does not hesitate to bite off any roots which get in its way and it therefore causes a great deal of damage for the farmer.

This little animal, only about 10 centimetres in length, can dig out about 15 metres of tunnel an hour, forming under the surface of the fields a whole network of holes, all leading to its den, which is shaped like a double circle with interconnecting passages.

A sure sign of the presence of moles in a field are the mole hills which appear over night where there was previously an expanse of green turf. Clear traces of its tunnels, dug between one mound and the next, can be seen just below the surface.

Why the rattle-snake is so called

The rattle-snake is one of the most poisonous snakes in America.

Fortunately the number of people bitten by these snakes is very small. They are not aggressive creatures and also the presence of a rattle-snake is easily detected because of the characteristic noise which it makes with its tail as it moves.

It is called a rattle-snake for that very reason. The rattle consists of a number of horny scales at the end of the tail which produce a jingle when they are shaken.

The ordinary rattle-snake which is found throughout the arid zones of North America, is about one and a half metres long. Its body temperature is dependent on external conditions and it adjusts its habits to avoid extreme temperatures. In hot weather it becomes nocturnal, lying hidden during the daytime in deep holes which it often digs for itself. It is becoming rather rare now because of the ferocity with which it was hunted.

It is a curious thing that in addition to shooting the rattle-snake owes its destruction to being hunted down by pigs which have no fear of its poison.

American rattle-snakes have a special organ between the nostrils and the eyes which enables them to detect the presence of warm-blooded animals even on the darkest night. It consists of two dimples which are extremely sensitive to heat. In a way it may be said that the rattle-snake possesses an organ like our modern infra-red ray detectors to identify its prey in the dark and pounce on it before it can flee.

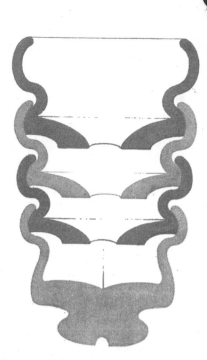

The sound of the rattle-snake is produced by the scales which form the tail. They are hollow and make the characteristic noise as they rub against one another.

Why the cheetah is easy to train

The speed which a cheetah can achieve when running is proverbial. When launched against its prey this cat can do more than 100 kilometres an hour, and it is therefore very difficult for any animal to escape when it is in pursuit. Gazelles, which are the prey it likes best, are themselves very agile and fast but they inevitably fall under the claws of the cheetah.

Once the victim is caught it is pulled to the ground and seized by the throat. But that is no reason for accusing the cheetah of ferocity. Indeed, among the large cats it is one of the least dangerous and kills only for food.

Not only does it never attack man but it is quite easy to tame and becomes as docile and gentle as a large cat.

Why the mayfly only lives a few hours

Large swarms of mayfly sometimes fly over stagnant water in light nuptual dances which precede the laying of the eggs.

They are slight, decliate insects about 2 millimetres long with four transparent wings and with two long trailers at the back.

They belong to the order Ephemeroptera and this Latin name indicates the basic character of their life, for what can be shorter and more brief than a life which lasts for only a few hours? Just time to lay their eggs and to fall to the ground exhausted.

For this reason the mayfly has no mouth when it is fully grown. The larvae may live for as long as two or three years in the water and provide good feeding for the fish which search for them in the mud at the bottom of the ponds.

Why ponds encourage the spread of mosquitoes

Ponds and swamps are favourite breeding places for mosquitoes.

Before coming to buzz around our houses, the mosquito goes through the larva stage in a pond where the eggs are laid. They may be deposited on the surface of the water or attached to floating plants.

The mosquito larvae have a strange way of breathing. Its head is down under the water but it pushes up above the water the opening of a slender tube, which is attached to the lower part of its body.

It uses this abdominal tube for taking in air from outside which it cannot do without.

Why gulls are fierce birds

Large, wild, proud birds, the gulls announce their presence as soon as they approach the coast by their high-pitched screeching and with their long, swooping flight they watch everything that happens along the beaches.

They are real scavengers and clear the coastline of all edible waste. There is no limit to their greed and daring, all in the search for food.

They often carry out raids on the nests of other birds and steal the eggs and the chicks. In other words they are out-and-out thieves, for whom one can have little sympathy. But to see them flying in the blue sky with their powerful wings and gay vivacity, one would never think of their fierce greed and would be charmed by the picture of power and elegance.

Why the magpie is said to be a thief

We shall probably never know why the magpie is a thief. He is particularly fond of shining objects, which reflect and sparkle. As soon as he gets possession of them he holds them fast in his beak, carries them up into the trees and hides them in crevices and in the most unlikely places.

Very often the nest becomes a storehouse of the most varied objects: spoons, spectacles, pieces of glass and coins. As the magpie lives near houses and dwellings he has innumerable chances of stealing anything he fancies. And as he is a bird which eats almost anything he is not short of food even in the winter, and so does not have to migrate. When the weather is bad the magpies collect in small groups and scour the countryside for something to eat.

Black-headed gulls

Why some snakes eat other snakes

Everyone knows that snakes are predators and meat-eaters: they are even able to swallow whole very large animals.

But perhaps not everyone knows that there are snakes which feed almost entirely on other snakes.

Among these are the coral snakes of the United States which have a tapered body covered with very bright scales.

The head is usually black and the whole of the body is decorated with yellow, red and black rings, which is why it is sometimes called the harlequin snake.

With such bright colouring it would be difficult for the coral snake to hide among the vegetation in wait for its prey. In fact, these snakes prefer to hide by digging in the ground or burying themselves in the sand.

The coral snake has a very powerful poison but it never uses it against man, of whom it is afraid. The poison is used to capture and stun other snakes on which it feeds.

This snake belongs to the same family as the cobra and other very poisonous snakes.

Why there are no longer any dinosaurs

The most famous prehistoric animals are certainly the dinosaurs, gigantic reptiles, some skeletons of which have been found and are preserved in museums. Their name means 'terrible lizard' and indicates that they were the largest and most terrifying animals on Earth.

The dinosaurs lived in the Mesozoic Era which covered the Triassic, Jurassic and Cretaceous Periods. They grew to gigantic and monstrous size and then, about 65 million years ago, they disappeared from the Earth.

The mystery of the dinosaurs' sudden disappearance has excited many scientists. Several different theories have been put forward, and one of the most convincing is that about 65 million years ago, a large asteroid collided with the Earth. There is geological evidence

to support the conclusion that such an event did happen at that time.

The result of the collisions could have been to raise millions of tons of dust into the atmosphere, producing a world-wide and long-lasting winter. The dinosaurs would not have been able to adapt themselves to this sudden change in climate and they would have died of cold or starvation.

They dominated the Earth for about 140 million years. Some were vegetarian and others fierce meat-eaters.

The majority of these reptiles lived in the fens and marshes but there were also some which lived in the water and some which could fly.

Why the honey-guide is so called

'Honey-guide' may seem a strange name for a bird but in this case no name is better deserved.

The honey-guide, which is a close relative of the woodpecker, is found mainly in Africa. It has a very refined taste in food and feeds only on honey and the larvae of wild bees.

Honey-guides have an infallible instinct which leads them to trees or crevices where there is a bees' nest but, once having found their eating-place, they are afraid to go in for fear of the violent reaction of the lawful owners.

What do they do then? They fly into the woods in search of some man or animal which likes honey, and by sound and movement attract his attention. They then guide him to the bees' nest they have discovered, and wait.

They know that the man or animal will empty the nest and take away the honey, but they also know that there will be a little left behind for them.

Ratel and man following a honeyguide

Asia. This animal is a really blood-thirsty one and it is not content, like the lion, to kill the victim which is going to supply it with a meal. Whenever it can it carries out a massacre among the herds and animals at the water-holes, just for the pleasure of seeing the blood flow.

If often happens that the female tiger, having given birth to five or six cubs, will eat the weak ones and leave only one or two, to which she will teach all the tricks of hunting.

When it grows old and loses its agility, the tiger becomes very dangerous and will even attack man.

Once in India and other parts of Asia tiger hunting was a common sport. These hunts were carried out on a large scale with hundreds of beaters and the hunters riding on tame elephants.

If it is captured young and raised in captivity the tiger can be tamed to some degree and an act with tigers is always a great attraction in the circus. However the tamer has always to be on the alert against any sudden outbreak of ferocity.

Why the tiger has a striped coat

The vertical yellow and black stripes of the tiger's fur act as a camouflage coat. It conceals the tiger among the bamboos and marsh vegetation of the places where it lives, particularly the jungles and lush undergrowth of

Why some animals hibernate

Let us take a look at the ground in the winter. When it is not covered with snow and ice it is hard and bare. There is not an insect to be seen and not a single fruit remains on the bare branches of the trees. Just imagine what a life of suffering it would be for many wild animals if nature had not arranged for them to fall asleep for several months.

And they go to sleep just at the right time. For some animals it is a matter of a heavy sleep with

brief interruptions for the needs of survival: this is what happens to the squirrel, for example, which even at the height of winter finds time to munch the acorns which he stored away in the summer.

In some cases, it is much more than that; the rhythm of life slows down for such animals just as it does for plants, the temperature falls, the blood flows slowly, the breathing slows down and becomes almost imperceptible. This state of almost complete quiet is called hibernation.

For reptiles, amphibians and some fish hibernation is even more total: for them the arrest of life is almost complete in winter.

During hibernation, of course, the animals consume the fats accumulated in the summer and when they awake again they have lost a good deal of weight

Why the chameleon often changes colour

A close relative of the lizard, the slow-worm and other reptiles, the chameleon does not live in our part of the world but it is common in the whole of Africa and in some parts of Asia, where there are about eighty species. It can grow to a length of 60 centimetres but the most common variety does not exceed 30 centimetres.

The most striking thing about the chameleon is the speed with which it can change colour, from white to yellow, to black, to green, to brown.

It is generally thought that the chameleon changes colour in order to match its background, but in fact these changes are due to the changes of light and temperature of its surroundings and the condition of the animal.

Indeed the chameleon has no need for camouflage because when it is out hunting it is able to deceive its prey by remaining perfectly still on a branch for hours. It is always sure of plenty to eat because of its sticky tongue which can dart out at its prey even to a distance of 10 centimetres.

The chameleon is well adapted for the life it leads in the trees. Its feet and tail are able to grasp a branch and hang there without difficulty when it is reaching out to capture some victim. The large prominent eyes can turn 180° and each one can move independently.

Chameleon

Why birds of prey are necessary for the balance of nature

In the country birds of prey have a bad reputation for stealing chickens and farm animals. The buzzard is a particular offender but when you get to know this bird better it turns out to be more useful than harmful.

It is about 60 centimetres in length and with a wing span of 120 centimetres; these are the average measurements for a buzzard which, because of its large

Red-tailed buzzard

size, can at first sight be mistaken for an eagle.

The expert, however, cannot mistake it for any other daytime bird of prey, even if it is merely a dot high in the sky. The buzzard has broad wings and a rounded tail and in its flight it traces wide characteristic spirals, searching with its keen eye the countryside below for signs of its prey.

The speed with which it dives down from the sky on to its

chosen victim is really astounding; it falls like a stone, with wings closed, and only opens them again just before touching down. The spectator hardly has time to see a sudden ruffling of feathers before the buzzard is climbing into the sky once more with a small mammal or reptile gripped tightly in its sharp talons.

It prefers mice and squirrels but it likes other small animals and does not hesitate to attack even a viper, although it is not immune against its poison.

For these reasons it should be regarded as a valuable ally of man.

Why the woodpecker remains in the woods during the winter

At the approach of the bad weather insects become scarcer and scarcer. The cold kills them off or forces them to hide away in sheltered places. That is why almost all insectivorous birds migrate in search of more plentiful food.

Common buzzard

Woodpecker

Two-toed sloth

Not the woodpecker, however; he remains in the woods and continues to peck away at the bark with his strong beak in search of food. This bird has a perfect knowledge of how to capture the larvae of insects inside the trunks, where they are hidden, and therefore he does not lack for food even in the winter.

When, by pecking with his beak, he finds that some larvae have made a tunnel, the woodpecker makes a hole with astonishing speed. He puts his long, sticky tongue into the hole and captures the larvae without hesitation so that it finishes in his capacious stomach.

It is easy to see how useful the woodpecker is in removing from the plants a large amount of larvae which are harmful for the wood. For this reason it is protected by law.

The woodpecker's nest is also very interesting; it is dug out in the shape of a bottle inside old dead tree trunks and the bottom is covered with soft wood shavings.

The sloth is a strange animal of equatorial America; indolent, lazy, incapable of any effort or initiative, it spends the whole of its life gripping with its long claws the branch of a large tree and eating all the leaves within reach of its mouth. Sloths move only when there is no more food and they have to find another leafy branch.

The females often rest hanging head downwards with the baby clinging to their rough fur of their stomachs. More rarely these animals sleep coiled up in the fork of a tree.

It is nevertheless always difficult to observe the sloth because its shaggy fur is of a grey-green colour which makes it resemble a shapeless lump of moss.

These creatures do not even come down to the ground to drink. Rather than do something so energetic they quench their thirst with the few drops of dew they can manage to lick from the leaves each night.

Generally silent, they can, when necessary, utter a shrill cry.

Why ducks have a beak with a serrated edge

Like all birds of the same family ducks have a very flat beak, the upper part of which has a serrated or saw edge. The reason for this is that it provides a fine filter which the bird uses for sifting the mud from the ponds in search of the lavae and small animals which are its food.

Ducks are aquatic birds with webbed feet and feathers waterproofed by oil from a gland near the tail. In the wild state they need a small area of water, not very deep, in which to wallow in search of food. For this reason they are usually to be found in marshes where they can merge readily against the background vegetation.

In the northern countries the wild ducks, especially the mallards, are very numerous but they only remain during the summer months and migrate to the south as soon as there is any threat of the ponds where they find their food becoming frozen.

A Mallard drake courting a hen Pintail

Why the dipper can go under water

Crafty and quick, the dipper (or water-ousel) looks like a large-size copy of the wren. He has a stocky body, small head, straight pointed beak, short wings, fan tail and dark plumage with a white throat and breast.

He likes to live near mountain torrents and his favourite perch is a stone lapped by the water, from which he can keep an eye on the bottom without appearing to do so, all the time whistling merrily. He can swim on the surface of the water, despite the fact that his feet are not webbed.

When he sees an insect, a shellfish or a young fish he dives into the water and goes right to the bottom to capture it. Any other bird which tried to imitate his actions would drown in a few seconds. But the body of the dipper is made in such a way as to enable him to dive.

As soon as he enters the water his nostrils are closed by two membranes and a special system of 'central heating' comes into action. His perfectly watertight plumage and reinforced cornea complete his submarine equipment.

The ease with which he goes down to the bottom of the water is also due to his ability to take advantage of the current.

He is so expert at this that he can even cross rapids and waterfalls. In order to keep his balance when the current is very swift he opens and shuts his small wings and uses his tail as a rudder.

The dipper feeds on water insects as well as on small crustaceans and molluscs which it catches under water.

Why the sole has both eyes on the same side

The sole is a timid and weak fish. It flattens itself out on the bottom of the sea and with a few strokes of its fins it covers itself with sand and even changes colour in order to hide better.

The most interesting thing about this timid fish·are the eyes, which are both situated on the same side of the head, one a little in front of the other.

When they are born in the open sea the larvae of the sole have normal eyes but gradually the left eye moves closer to the other eye, and it is a good thing that it does so. What use would the sole make of an eye on the left side of its body when this is destined to remain all the time resting on the sea bed?

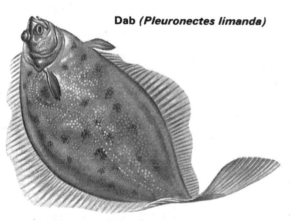

Dab (Pleuronectes limanda)

Sole (Solea solea)

Why the griffon vulture appears on many coats of arms

The griffon vulture is the most arrogant member of a family of birds of prey common in Europe and southern Asia.

It is included on many of the coats of arms of noble families because with its haughty bearing it is the very symbol of pride and power.

This bird is about a metre long and like all vultures of the old world has a short powerful face, large and rounded wings and very powerful talons. It also has extremely sharp eyesight.

It can be distinguished from other birds of prey by the neck and head which are completely covered in white down. The young ones have a circle of dark feathers at the base of the neck but this turns white when they are fully grown.

The griffon is rather awkward on the ground but it is an expert flyer, wheeling and circling with effortless grace while searching for food. It prefers solitary peaks but it is also frequently seen near villages where there is easy prey. That is why it was hunted down with poisoned bait and has now disappeared from many areas. Yet the scavenging of vultures is invaluable in the control of pollution and disease, and for this reason vultures are protected by law in many countries.

The griffon builds its nest of twigs in crevices of the rocks and in trees or lays its single egg in an abandoned nest. The male and female birds take it in turns to hatch the egg for fifty days and then they both feed the young one with the flesh of birds and mammals.

Why the hedgehog is not afraid of vipers

The hedgehog is a small mammal, about 25 centimetres long, which is found in Europe, Asia and parts of Africa. It deserves a little more consideration and respect than it receives for it is very useful to the farmer, destroying insects and vipers.

But ignorance is a great enemy of civilization and although people are grateful to the hedgehog for the services it does them, all too often when they see one in the fields, they hasten to kill it as they would any other vermin.

It would be better to let the hedgehog wander through the fields because it hunts moles, insects, vermin and, in particular, the viper.

It is not afraid of the viper's bite. Hedgehogs have been seen to let vipers bite them on the nose. They play with them as a cat plays with a mouse and then swallow them whole.

It is known that when the hedgehog senses danger it rolls up into a ball and offers to its enemy an impenetrable barrier of quills which discourages all attack.

It hibernates during the winter, rolled up in a nest of dry leaves.

Why some birds migrate

This is a question to which no completely satisfactory answer has yet been found. The search for food and a mild climate is the chief reason, but there are some strange and mysterious things about these migrations. How is it, for instance, that the Arctic tern always spends the summer in the Arctic polar regions and then goes to spend the winter in the Antarctic, covering each year a distance of 35,000 kilometres on the return journey, when only a very short journey would bring it to more hospitable places?

Why do some birds prefer to lengthen their journey by thousands of kilometres to avoid obstacles, while others are not afraid to cross oceans or pass directly over mountain chains, flying at heights of more than 9,000 metres.

That a bird born and reared in our climate senses at a certain time the approach of bad weather and knows by instinct that it must flee for safety to a more hospitable region, is a fact that arouses admiration.

That without any guide they are able to fly over mountains and seas and reach the temperate regions of the south where their parents lived in previous years, is even more astounding.

That in the end they are able not only to find the way back again but also reach the same pond, the same waterfall, the same nest where they were born, is indeed a miraculous fact.

It is easy in these cases to talk about instinct. But how is it possible that instinct alone can guide the golden plover on a journey of 30,000 kilometres from the Arctic areas to Argentina and back again? A journey fraught

with difficulties. And, moreoever, how do some birds find their way when they travel on dark nights without a moon in order to avoid the traps of their enemies? How do the petrels find their way when they prefer to travel on foggy days?

It is known that migrating birds are able to change direction suddenly to avoid contrary winds or hurricanes; in other words they know how to find the way to their winter quarters by another route. How is this possible?

Despite intensive research by many scientists, these and other aspects of bird migration have not yet been explained satisfactorily.

(above) Main routes of migration of swallows
(below) Migration routes from the North Pole southwards

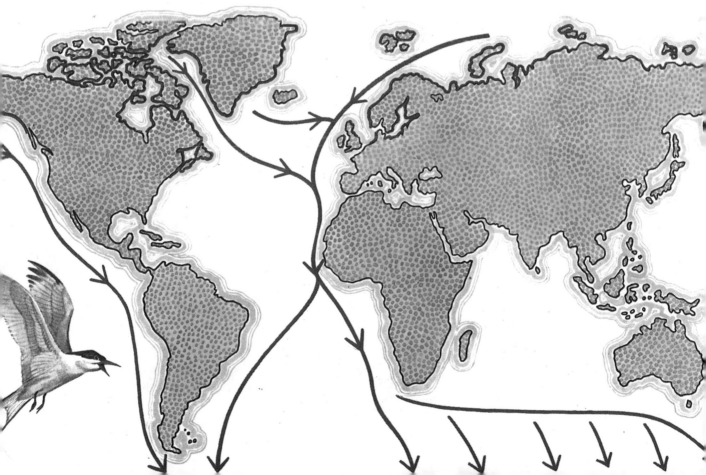

THE WHY OF MAN

Why it is possible to find very old skeletons

Archaeologists and particularly those who are interested in the problems of ancient burials, often come across skeletons in a very good state of preservation. This is because human bones are composed for the most part of two mineral substances: phosphorus and calcium. It is in fact the calcium which gives the bones their strength and whiteness.

Skeletons rarely disintegrate completely although not all the 206 bones which make up our bodies remain intact. The parts of the skeleton which are usually best preserved include the skull together with the lower jaw. Other bones which are normally well preserved, in addition to the skull, are the long bones of the limbs, the ribs and the pelvis.

Why complete sets of teeth are rarely found

Although teeth are really bones, perhaps even more solid than the skeleton, it is extremely rare that a complete set of teeth is found among the remains of ancient man.

There can be many reasons why teeth are missing; some will be the result of disease and some the result of accidents and fractures.

We know for certain that the habit which was very common among the ancients of eating certain types of food containing a kind of mould, was the cause of widespread dental decay.

In addition, of course, primitive man was very often in danger of losing his teeth: fights with animals, falls, the effort of chewing very hard foods all contributed to this.

Why man walks on two legs

Walking on two legs is something we do quite naturally, without stopping to think that it is a most difficult thing to achieve. Indeed, it requires a great sense of balance and correct control of the muscles. Standing erect and walking are acts typical of man and of no other animal. Even the apes, which of all living animals are most like man, walk differently.

If we compare the human foot with that of a gorilla, there are two very obvious differences. First of all the human foot, contrary to that of the apes, has a flat base; secondly the ape has a big toe which can be moved opposite to the other toes so that it can grip curved surfaces such as the branches of trees.

The feet, indeed, are an indication of the kind of life that these two creatures lead. Man needs to stand erect and walk and the apes to grip the branches of trees and to leap from one to another.

able to build enormous constructions as well as very small ones, to play musical instruments, to cut, manipulate and to put food into his mouth.

Why the human hand is able to do all kinds of work

It is said that man's first tool is his hand. No-one pays much attention to such an obvious remark, yet if we remember the difficulties we suffer when, for example, we have a hand in plaster, we realize how much we depend on this essential part of the human body.

What makes it possible for the hand to perform such a wide variety of actions is above all the thumb. It can 'oppose itself' to the other fingers and enable the hand to tie things, to grasp and to pick up objects.

Because of his hands man is

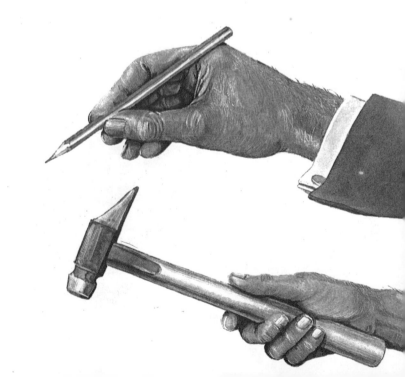

Why primitive man made implements of stone

In this age of technical progress in which we live, it is not only interesting but perhaps also profitable to discover the tools which our remote ancestors used for their work and the weapons with which they defended themselves.

The first tools and weapons were made of stone; they are still found today by the thousand in places where ancient man once lived. To us they seem insignificant pieces of flint but to primitive man they often represented his only means of survival. He had to spend day after day in the task of detaching them from the rocks, sharpening and polishing them so that they could be used for cutting, scraping, striking, skinning, digging and removing bones.

However simple and crude these first implements of man may appear when we see them in museums, they represent a great step forward in the progress of mankind.

Why primitive man painted the walls of his caves

From all the evidence we have it appears that primitive man also had the urge to create wonderful things out of his imagination. In Spain, France, the Sahara and Sicily we can still admire these scratchings and paintings on the walls of caves which were done some 30,000 years ago.

Bison, horses, deer and mammouths drawn or painted by the first human artists still astonish those who see them by their remarkable power and realism.

One thing stands out among many others: the often repeated drawing of the human hand.

Ancient man was already so aware of the importance of his first 'tool' that he saw in it something magical and mysterious and he therefore liked to reproduce it in the paintings and drawings with which he decorated his cave.

Why man and apes may have the same origin

This is a very old question which has divided scientists who study the origin of man into two camps.

Some believe that they can explain the true origin of man on a physical basis: that is to say that man is the result of a process of evolution which in the course of millions of years transformed the body of one type of ape into the present human body.

Chemical examinations which required very long and specialized study, appear to have established that the structural differences between human blood and the blood of the man-like apes are very small.

Obviously the time required for the human body to acquire its present form has to be measured in millions of years: according to some theories, between 5 and 30 million years.

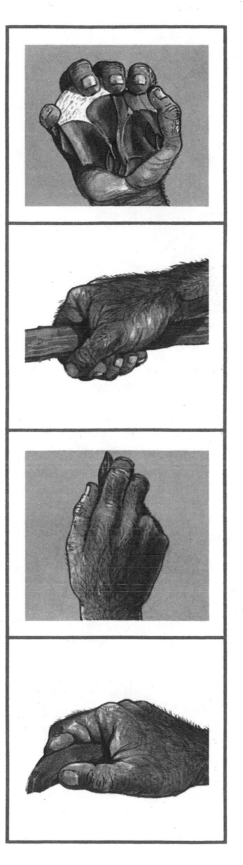

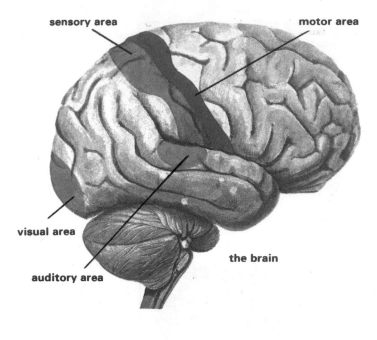

sensory area
motor area
visual area
auditory area
the brain

Why it is the brain which controls the body

According to old beliefs and superstitions the various human emotions were located in particular parts of the body: courage, for instance, resided in the heart, cowardice was connected with the liver, cunning with the brain, hatred with the bile, and so on.

Although it is possible to find some truth in such ideas, science has definitely established that the brain is the organ which controls all our actions without exception, and the brain is therefore the control centre of the body.

How does this come about?

The brain and the spinal cord, which is the natural continuation of the brain, are made of a very delicate and rather soft material, grey in colour, which occupies the whole of the skull and the long central core of the backbone. Special channels and nerves lead into this very sensitive material and it is their task to transmit to the brain all the sensations received from the various sense organs and then to pass on at once the orders which the brain sends to the organs, even to the farthest limits of the body.

The nervous system, the headquarters of which is the brain, is responsible, therefore, for all our actions: seeing, hearing, smelling, tasting and touching. But it is above all due to the nervous system, and therefore to the brain, that we are able to appreciate and understand our senses.

When we talk about mental health, nervous diseases and depression we are concerned with the nervous system. Nowadays medicine has become very specialized in the field of nervous diseases because it is considered, and rightly so, that as a result of the hectic life which modern man leads, it represents one of the most delicate areas of medicine and one subject to the greatest changes.

The weight of the brain varies

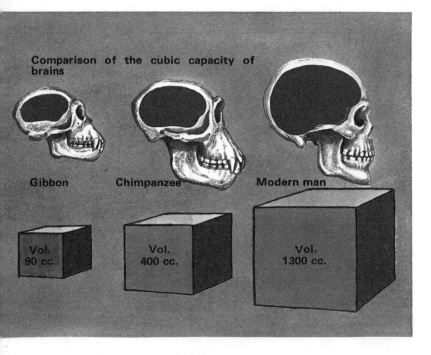

Comparison of the cubic capacity of brains

Gibbon
Vol. 90 cc.

Chimpanzee
Vol. 400 cc.

Modern man
Vol. 1300 cc.

with age, height, body weight, sex and race.

The brain of the adult man is heavier than that of a woman, in this country averaging 1,409 grammes as compared with 1,263 grammes.

The two hemispheres into which it is divided are symmetrical but although they are identical they do not have identical functions: various sense or motor activities are located at different points and sometimes in only one of the hemispheres. For instance, the centre of language, of the association between written words and spoken words, between ideas and the words which represent them, are normally only located in the left hemisphere and therefore these faculties are not impaired if for some reason the right hemisphere is injured.

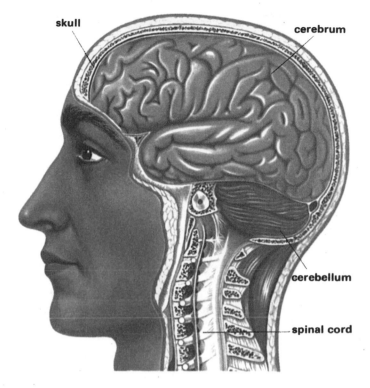

skull

cerebrum

cerebellum

spinal cord

Why we say that an intelligent person is brainy

The current sayings regarding the brain, such as 'brainless' or 'very brainy' to describe people of little intelligence or of great intelligence, may seem to be merely ordinary phrases or old superstitions but nevertheless there is some truth in these sayings. That part of the brain where ideas are formed, where the memory is located and where our free choice is decided is much more developed in man than in any other animal, living or long dead.

The average weight of the human brain is about 1,300 grammes. The animal which in proportion to size has a brain nearest to man's is the chimpanzee with a brain weighing about 400 grammes.

Why it is important to protect the back of the neck

The part of the brain situated at the back is called the cerebellum. Its location at the back and below the skull is a very delicate one as it coincides with the place where the skull and the backbone meet.

Artificial protection of this part of the head has always been a problem; for instance, in time of war special helmets were used to protect the nape of the neck.

Why go to so much trouble? Because the cerebellum has the delicate task of co-ordinating the movements of the muscles and keeping them in a state of readiness to carry out whatever orders they may be given, whether it is a delicate task, some simple operation or the rapid movements of self defence.

Why we have a skeleton

The movements of the body are carried out by special bundles of flesh called muscles. However, the complex muscular system would not be able to function at all if it were not supported by a suitable structure. This structure is the skeleton. It is in reality a kind of framework which supports the body.

Although this description is correct to a certain extent it is not the whole story. First of all because the skeleton is a framework which is capable of very complex movements, quite different from ordinary frameworks; in the second place because the function of supporting the body is not the sole purpose of the skeleton. The bones are not only more or less strong supports, well and efficiently jointed together, but they are also living elements of our bodies, organs which are entrusted with delicate tasks.

In the central cavity of almost all bones, for instance, there is a soft tissue known as the bone marrow, which in the long bones has the task of producing the red and white cells of the blood. Although they appear solid the bones are penetrated by a large number of tiny holes through which pass the blood vessels which feed the bones themselves.

Fewer but larger vessels also pass through to collect from the marrow the blood cells just mentioned and put them into circulation.

Since the tasks of the skeleton are so important and delicate it is easy to understand the advice doctors give to all, but particularly to the young, to enrich their diet with calcium and phosphorus, without which the bones would become either too fragile or too hard.

Why a splint has to be put on a broken limb

How can a broken bone become strong and firm again? Because it is a living part of the body and it is therefore unlike metals or minerals which cannot grow together again once they are broken. Human bones are, in fact, made of both inorganic and organic substances and the latter possess the ability to reproduce their cells, albeit slowly, until the damaged tissue is healed.

Sometimes, a further layer of bone is even created at the site of the fracture. For this reconstruction to take place it is essential that the limb or damaged part is immobilized. That is why plaster of Paris casts or splints are applied to the injured limb.

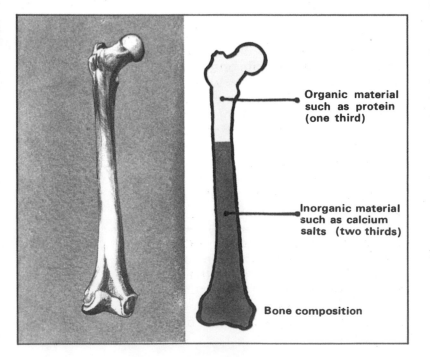

Organic material such as protein (one third)

Inorganic material such as calcium salts (two thirds)

Bone composition

Why sport is good for us

Physical activity brings into play the muscles which develop in various ways according to how we use them. For instance, a boxer will have well developed arm muscles and a footballer will have good leg muscles.

The activity of the muscles also varies with what we do during the day: during the time we devote to study, the muscles of the eyes and hands will be most used but when we are moving about it will be the muscles of the limbs and abdomen, and so on.

Sport is therefore a safety-valve because among other things it is a way of exercising all the muscles of our bodies together and making sure that some of them are not left too long inactive. This is why the so-called complete sports, such as tennis, athletics and swimming, are to be recommended.

Why our bodies can perform such a variety of movements

If the bones of the skeleton were all fixed solidly together the body would not be capable of any movement at all.

In fact, however, we know that we are capable at any given moment of making all kinds of movements. This is made possible by the various joints which we have in our bodies.

Some of these joints permit only a relatively limited movement. In the spine or backbone, for example, each vertebra can only make slight movements because it is prevented by hard ligaments of fibrous tissue which serve as a protective cover.

On the other hand the most mobile joints are those of the legs, arms, hands and fingers: the joints of the knees and fingers are like hinges and those of the elbows like pivots.

The most mobile of all are the ball and socket joints of the shoulders and hips.

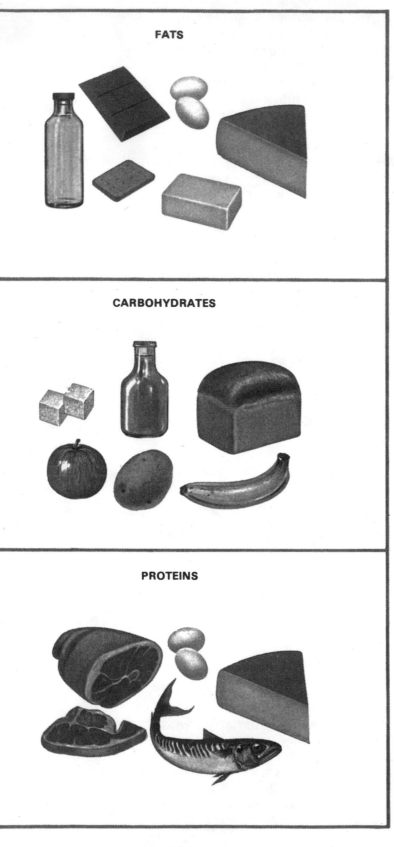

FATS

CARBOHYDRATES

PROTEINS

Why our bodies need food

In order to be always efficient and do their work properly the cells which form our bodies need certain vital substances: carbohydrates.

These are made up of three chemical elements: carbon, oxygen and hydrogen. The human organism converts the carbohydrates into sugars to enable the cells to utilize them. To make a very ordinary comparison, sugar is for our bodies what petrol is for our cars: fuel.

In addition to sugar our organism needs other very important substances: fats and proteins. The first, weight for weight, supplies twice as much food value as the sugar.

Carbohydrates, fats and proteins are found in plentiful amounts in the foods we eat every day. Eating is therefore a prime necessity for man as it supplies his organism with the energy to enable it to function correctly.

The amount of energy which various foods provide has been measured by scientists in special units called calories. A calorie is the amount of heat required to raise 1 kilogram of water 1°C. The human body needs varying numbers of calories according to the work it has to do. For example, if 3,000 calories a day are enough for light work, at least 4,500 calories are needed for heavy work.

It should be remembered, moreover, that the nutrition which comes from foods, particularly from fats, serves not only for immediate use but also to provide stores of energy to be used as and when required. To function properly, however, our bodies require regular, well-balanced meals.

Why vitamins are essential to life

There is one type of food which the body cannot do without: the vitamins. They were quite unknown not so very long ago but they constitute an essential part of our daily food and without them the body can suffer considerable damage. The lack of vitamin A, for instance, is the cause of eye diseases and skin diseases; a shortage of vitamin B gives rise to nervous troubles; insufficient vitamin C can cause scurvy and vitamin D deficiency is the direct cause of rickets in young children. Rickets is indeed one of the commonest diseases in those parts of the world where food is scarce.

A correctly balanced intake of vitamins, therefore, provides the body with the best conditions of health and an improved nervous system.

Why alcohol is a poison

Although wines and other alcoholic drinks are in daily use, often in quite large amounts, it must be remembered that alcohol can be dangerous.

This is primarily because it is not a food and cannot therefore be used for the 'fuelling' of the body, nor is it transformed into a natural reserve like some foods which are converted into reserves of fat.

In addition, even as a source of energy alcohol is an inferior product because it acts as a violent stimulant and has a harmful effect on the balance of the organism.

Alcohol should, therefore, be taken in moderation and at the right times, for instance, with meals.

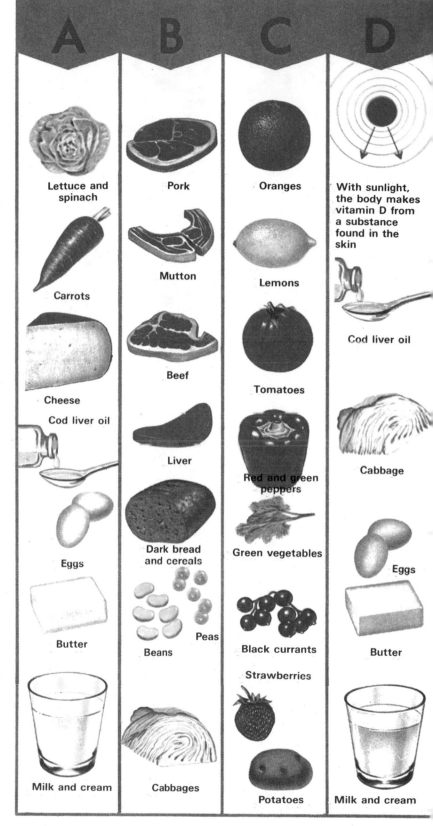

Some sources of the principle vitamins

A
Lettuce and spinach
Carrots
Cheese
Cod liver oil
Eggs
Butter
Milk and cream

B
Pork
Mutton
Beef
Liver
Dark bread and cereals
Beans
Peas
Cabbages

C
Oranges
Lemons
Tomatoes
Red and green peppers
Green vegetables
Black currants
Strawberries
Potatoes

D
With sunlight, the body makes vitamin D from a substance found in the skin
Cod liver oil
Cabbage
Eggs
Butter
Milk and cream

Human sex determination

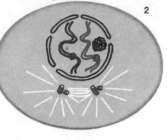

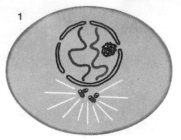

(1 and 2)
Prophase: the chromosomes extend and the two halves move apart

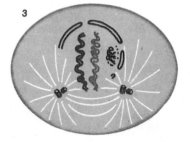

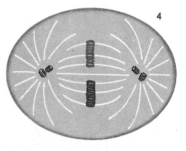

(3 and 4)
Metaphase: the membrane disappears and the chromosomes move to opposite poles of the cell

(5 and 6)
Anaphase: the chromosomes are each divided into two chromatids

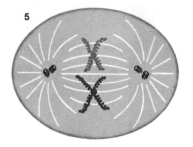

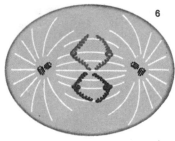

(7 and 8)
Telophase: each chromatid of every chromosome migrates towards one pole and the full duplication of the cell takes place

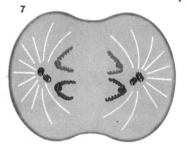

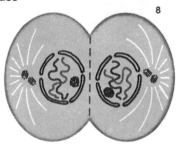

Why cells multiply

All the cells of the body originate in the fertilized egg but when a baby is born its body consists of about 200,000 million cells.

The process of cell multiplication is a complex but very interesting one. It can be put briefly like this: the fertilized cell has a nucleus or centre which quickly divides into two. The two new nuclei slowly move apart to opposite ends of the cell. The filaments or slender threads which form the chromosomes divide lengthwise, each forming two segments. Thus divided, the chromosomes also separate into two groups, each containing an equal number of parts and move towards opposite poles of the cell and arrange themselves near each nucleus. The cell slowly divides to form two new cells.

The process is repeated with the new cells, which divide in turn, starting off a multiple chain reaction.

Why a baby has to have both a father and a mother

The human body is an extraordinarily perfect machine, able to perform delicate and complex tasks, capable of reproducing continuously the cells of damaged or worn-out tissues.

This would not be enough for the continuation of life if the human body were not also endowed with another wonderful function: that of creating other living beings, other organisms identical to itself.

This function requires the union of two individuals of opposite sex, a man and a woman. They each have cell producing organisms which fulfil a reproductive function: the female cell is called the ovum and the male cell is called the spermatozoon. When a spermatozoon penetrates an ovum and fertilizes it, it is the beginning of a new life.

Why children are like their parents

The ovum and the spermatozoon are very different both in size and function although their nuclei contain the same number of chromosomes. These are very fine filaments to which scientists give the letters X and Y; women have X chromosomes only and men have either X or Y chromosomes.

When the male and female cells unite, if both have X chromosomes the child will be female but if the male cell has Y chromosomes the child will be male. It is, therefore, the father's cell which determines the sex of a child.

More female babies are born than male ones although according to the laws of probability their numbers should be equal.

As regards the much discussed question of the resemblance between children and parents, it should be noted that the chromosomes contain genes, which are units which carry the physical and mental characteristics of each individual.

When the male and female cells combine and the chromosomes come together some physical and mental characteristics of each parent are transmitted to the child which is being formed. But children are not exact duplicates of their parents and normally differ from them in many respects.

Why everyone has a navel

The foetus has to be given nourishment in the mother's womb for a period of about nine months. Already by the fourth week it has the basic form of the child which will be born.

The embryo is fed by the nutritive substances in the mother's

Human sex determination

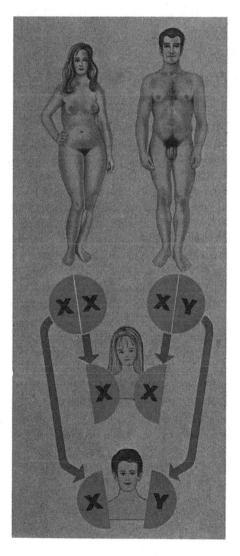

blood. These substances reach the embryo through the placenta, a kind of bag attached to the uterus.

The placenta is a special organ which serves to join together the mother's blood circulation and that of the embryo. It is connected to the child by means of the umbilical cord containing the blood vessels which are essential for feeding the baby.

At birth this cord is cut and that is why every one of us has a kind of round scar, the navel or umbilicus on the abdomen, which was the point where the cord was connected.

Why we must wash often with soap

In order to remain efficient, the human body needs to eliminate the harmful waste materials which it produces. Gas, water vapour and replacement tissues are continuously being expelled in large amounts through the lungs and kidneys. The skin also expels harmful substances although to a lesser extent.

How does this come about? The surface of the body is very rich in tiny tubes which end in small holes called pores. It is through these pores that the respiration of the skin continuously takes place.

If we covered all our body with a waterproof substance, a varnish for example, after a few hours we would cease to live, poisoned by the harmful substances which were unable to escape.

Dirt is the most frequent cause of poor respiration of the skin and therefore by washing ourselves often, not only hands and face but the whole body, we both preserve our health from danger of infection and also provide our body with the best conditions for efficiency.

Why the heart beats

A perfect system for watering the fields is an arrangement of canals which carry water from a single source of supply to every small patch of land. The number of channels becomes greater and the size of the channels becomes smaller the farther one goes from the source to the outside plain.

The same thing takes place in our bodies with regard to the circulation of the blood: from the heart, which is the main organ of circulation, large blood vessels, the arteries, branch out and these divide into a more and more extensive network of other vessels of smaller calibre. These smaller blood vessels reach the very extremities of the body and are called capillaries, because they are as thin as hairs. But the circulation of the blood is doubled for other channels, called veins, carry the blood from the periphery back to the heart.

The most important task in this continuous circulation of blood is that of the heart which is really a suction and compression pump. It begins to move blood through the baby's developing tissues months before birth and goes on working until death. Each heart beat performs a colossal task: every 24 hours the heart pumps about 12,000 litres of blood.

Why the blood is red

There is a special reason for the circulation of the blood in our body and that is the distribution to every cell of nutritive substances and oxygen and the removal of waste cell tissue.

The circulation of oxygen, a gas

which is vital to our organism, is the task of a special blood protein, haemoglobin, which is distinguished by its red colour. It is easy to see that this colour is not constant.

The explanation is a simple one: haemoglobin passes through the alveoli or air spaces of the lungs and becomes charged with oxygen which gives it a fine red colour; it is then carried by the blood into all the tissues and cells, to which it gives up its oxygen and thereby loses a good deal of its bright colour.

Why we need to breathe

Both steam engines and internal combustion engines, after burning the fuel they use, have to expel the gases resulting from combustion.

Our bodies behave in a rather similar way. By the movement of breathing in we absorb air which contains the oxygen essential for life.

At this point the lungs perform a delicate operation, that of extracting the oxygen from the air and passing it on to the blood. In turn the oxygenated blood spreads throughout the whole body, feeding the cells and collecting their waste tissues.

Returning to the lungs the blood gives up the waste material which is expelled when we breathe out.

To breathe means, therefore, two important operations: to take in oxygen and get rid of harmful gases. That is why the breathing of polluted air can cause serious damage and why there is so much concern about air pollution at the present time.

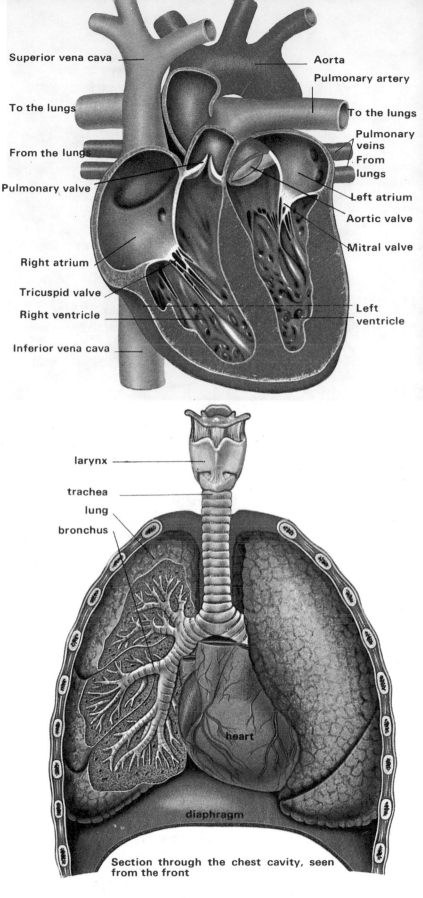

Superior vena cava — Aorta — Pulmonary artery — To the lungs — To the lungs — Pulmonary veins — From lungs — From the lungs — Pulmonary valve — Left atrium — Aortic valve — Mitral valve — Right atrium — Tricuspid valve — Right ventricle — Left ventricle — Inferior vena cava

larynx — trachea — lung — bronchus — heart — diaphragm

Section through the chest cavity, seen from the front

71

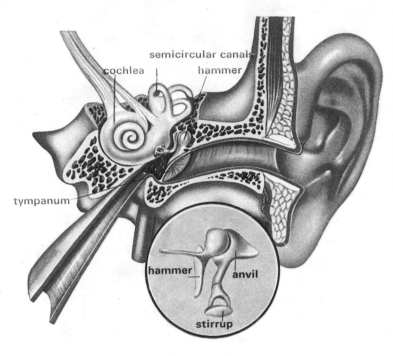

cochlea
semicircular canals
hammer
tympanum

hammer   anvil

stirrup

The stirrup transmits the vibra-tions to a special fluid which fills the inner ear. In turn the waves in the fluid pass them on to the cochlea which contains the funda-mental organ of hearing: the semicircular canals.

Among other things, these canals, in conjunction with the brain, enable us to keep our balance and to stand upright. The sound is finally transmitted to the brain by means of the acoustic nerve.

If the membrane of the ear drum is injured or there is any damage to the delicate apparatus of the ear, the hearing is impaired or lost altogether.

Nowadays, special hearing aids are available to correct defects of hearing.

Why we are able to hear sounds

We are able to receive messages which come to us from the outside world through our senses.

The messages which reach us by means of air waves are captured by the sense of hearing, which is located in the ear. The ear is a system of perfect mechanisms, closely connected with one another, which enables us to appreciate a wide range of tones and sounds.

By what means does this come about?

The sound waves are collected by the auricle, which is the part of the ear you can see, and cause the drum to vibrate; this is a very thin and taut membrane. The vibration produces movements of the tiny bones of the middle ear, which have rather curious names because of their shapes: hammer, anvil and stirrup.

Why we see the shapes and colours of objects

We see by means of the eyes. The eye is a very delicate and complex organ and works more or less like a camera.

Light enters the eye through a hole, the pupil; passes through a lens, the crystalline lens; is pro-jected on to a layer of special tissue, the retina, situated on the opposite wall of the eyeball. The retina functions like a photographic film and is modified by light; it is a very thin layer of nerve cells, called cones and rods, which identify the colour or black and white images. When light strikes the cones and rods the eye transmits to the optic nerve a detailed message of what it sees. The message reaches the brain, which at once gives the necessary instructions. The eye turns the images upside down in the same way as happens in a camera, and the brain reverses them once again so that we see them exactly as they are.

The special shape of the eye and the number of rods in the retina enable us to see the images of the external world in the usual way, but if the number of rods or the curvature of the retina were different, we would see things differently, as is indeed the case with some mammals. For example we know that the cow sees objects much larger than we see them and some members of the cat family are able to see in the dark because of the different shape of their eyes.

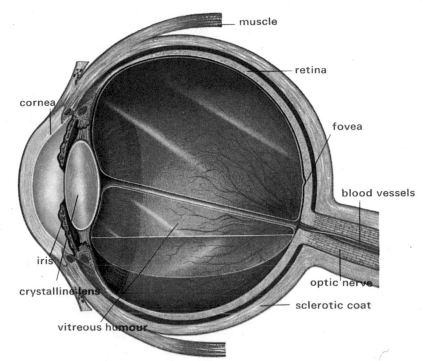

Why some people need spectacles

Quite different from glass lenses, the crystalline lens of the eye has the ability to alter its curvature. In fact it is provided with muscles which make it more spherical when it is looking at near objects and flatter when it has to look at distant objects. It may happen with the passage of time or through some other cause, that the crystalline lens loses some of its elasticity and the muscles are no longer able to change the curvature. The eye then sees near objects in a blurred manner. This defect is called presbyopia.

Whereas normal eyes see well both at long and short distances, there can be two cases where the diameter of the eyeball is not normal: myopia and hyperopia. Myopia is when the distance between the lens and the retina is too great and the eye can see near objects well but not distant ones. The reverse to this is hyperopia when the distance between the lens and the retina is too short and the eye sees distant objects and not those near at hand.

It is only in the last few centuries that the invention of special lenses for correcting vision has made it possible to help those with defective vision. Today a larger number of lenses are available for correcting almost any visual defect. A recent development is contact lenses: these are invisible when worn and give a wider field of vision than spectacles do.

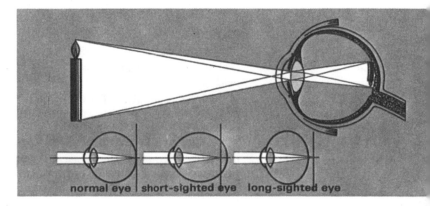

normal eye | short-sighted eye | long-sighted eye

Why we need to sleep

The physical and mental activity which our bodies perform every day cannot go on without a break.

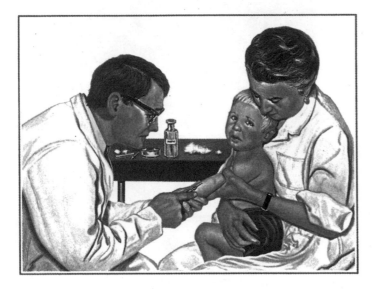

Like all machines, the body also needs to rest sometimes. Nor is physical rest alone able to give the body back its lost energy; the whole organism, including the mind, needs rest. We therefore require regular periods of sleep.

It is usual for man and many animals to sleep lying down. We can fall asleep sitting in a chair or even, when very tired, standing up. Some animals regularly sleep in a standing position.

As we sleep our muscles relax and stretch, the heart slows down and our mind has a rest from its continuous work.

Rest is just as essential as food and more important than medicines or tonics. Our grandparents knew this when they told us to sleep at least 8 hours every night.

Today we know that even this length of time is not enough for some people but is a reasonable average time.

Why vaccination is necessary against some diseases

In order to keep the body healthy and efficient it is wise, among other things, to submit to certain prescribed vaccinations.

The reason is a simple one; the human organism is constantly under attack by foreign bodies of various types which are called antigens. The organism reacts spontaneously to these attacks by producing antibodies. These wage furious war on the antigens and neutralize them.

Natural immunization, however, involves a very grave risk of the antigens prevailing over the antibodies.

For the past two centuries science has made available to doctors a series of vaccines against particular diseases. The purpose of vaccination is to produce artificially immunizing antibodies by injecting certain antigens into the body. Immunization was first used against smallpox, but it is now also used for diptheria, typhoid, poliomyelitis, measles and so on.

Why the electrocardiograph is used on patients with heart diseases

It is often said that all inventions of science complete and supplement one another in turns. This is very true in the field of medicine, from the study and preparation of drugs to surgery and from diagnosis to therapy. An example of this is the contribution made to scientific research by electronics when applied to the building of apparatus for checking the efficiency of our bodies.

The electrocardiograph is one of these machines. It records on a graph the electrical impulses arising in the human body as a result of successive contractions of the heart muscles. Specialists are able to read the electrocardiogram, that is the results of the examination of the heart by means of the electrocardiograph, and to identify the heart disease of the patient under examination.

In this way it is possible to operate in time to cure arrhythmias, which are changes of the heart rhythm, infarcts or injuries to the heart caused by arterial obstruction, and many other diseases of the circulatory system.

Why the electroencephalograph is used in some cases

Another electronic device built specially to help medical science is the electroencephalograph.

As the name indicates this instrument is intended for use in research into the human brain (encephalon). The electroencephalogram is the graphic recording which is obtained by means of the electroencephalograph of all the phenomena arising in the brain of man.

This recording is obtained by fixing to various parts of the head silver electrodes which are connected to a special recording device called an oscillograph. The recording is studied by specialists and provides them with very valuable indications on which to base their diagnosis and the treatment required.

These tests are usually made in cases of patients who show symptoms of mental disease, severe headaches and so on. It would be a good thing if everyone had these tests periodically to guard against sudden illness and obtain treatment in time.

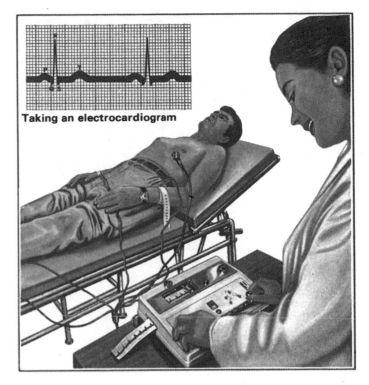

Taking an electrocardiogram

An E.E.G. machine in use

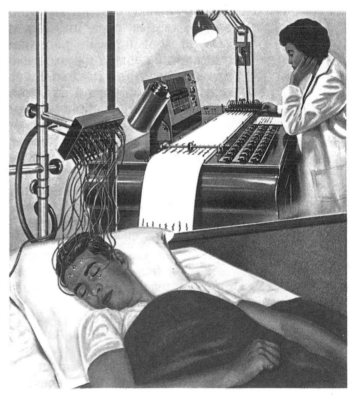

THE WHY OF WAR

Why rich men went to war in armour

Armour was a kind of personal defence, protective clothing made of materials which would withstand the blows of the enemy. The earliest forms of armour were made of animal skins, then of leather and later of metal. In the Middle Ages iron mail armour was introduced which allowed greater freedom of movement and was therefore preferred by those who fought on horseback. The horses were protected by special armour called bards.

It was not until the end of the fifteenth century that armour made entirely of steel came into use. It was at that time in particular that armour became the exclusive privilege of the few. Indeed it was only kings, nobles and rich men who were able to afford armour and have the luxury of being better protected in war; also the limited number of armourers worked only for those who could pay them well.

The head was specially protected by a helmet: it was made of the same material as the armour but fitted better. On the helmet could often be seen the insignia of rank. The face was protected by movable visors which were both strong and practical.

Why old cities had walls

Men have devised means of attack and defence against their enemies since the early days when they first fought among themselves.

One of the oldest methods invented by man to protect not only human life but also his dwellings and possessions, were the city walls. These were massive erections which can measure more than 10 metres at the base and rise to two to three times that height.

They were intended to place an insuperable obstacle in the way of the enemy and were often built very simply without any special embellishment; sometimes they were very rough indeed. They surrounded the city completely or at least the important centre of the city, and were often also surrounded by a deep moat filled with water. The oldest had scarcely any openings other than the entrance gate. At a later date long narrow slits were made in the walls from which the enemy could be attacked while the defenders remained well covered.

On the tops of the walls there were often ramparts where the soldiers could keep watch on the enemy and, in case of attack, occupy a good position overlooking their opponents. People were able to enter or leave the city by drawbridges located opposite the main gates.

These defensive city walls were of such solid construction that even today many of them are still in a perfect state of preservation. The greatest and most famous of all is the Great Wall of China which defends not merely a city but a whole vast country.

Why old cities were besieged

Against fortified cities the methods of attack were above all assault and siege.

Assault was an attempt to occupy the city by force by breaching the walls, by tunnels or by exploding mines. The idea of a siege was to force the city to surrender through lack of munitions or, more often, through lack of food.

For this purpose the first task of the besiegers was completely to surround the city and prevent anyone from entering or leaving. This was extremely important because anyone who left might get reinforcements or escape, neither of which the attackers wanted. Anyone going in could do even more damage by bringing help in some way to the besieged, particularly food and munitions.

The object of sieges was to force the enemy to yield and therefore an essential task of the besiegers was to weaken the resistance of the defenders within the walls.

In the course of history there have been some very famous sieges, some lasting for years. Perhaps the most famous was the siege of Troy which continued for ten years and was only ended by the stratagem of Ulysses, when the Trojans allowed the famous wooden horse within their walls.

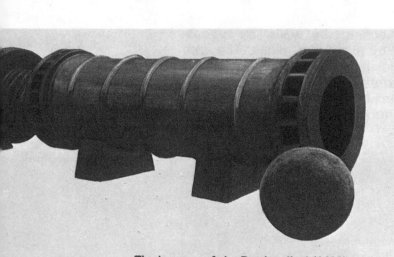

The 'cannon of the Dardanelles' (1464)

The catapult,
an old siege weapon

Why gunpowder was used for war

One of the problems which man had to solve from the time when he first began to hunt was that of finding weapons which could hit a target from a distance. The more afraid animals became of man, the further away from him they kept.

This led to the creation of various weapons which were thrown, and then to the bow and arrow.

The invention of gunpowder, that is a mixture of potassium nitrate, sulphur and carbon which burns very rapidly when it is lighted, led to a whole series of discoveries and finally to the firearm. This was a metal tube

One of the most spectacular self-propelled guns ever built was the German *Mrs Karl 040*. This vehicle was over 10 metres long and mounted a gun of 540 or 660 millimetre calibre. This monster was used at Sebastopol during the Russian campaign and at the end of the war in the unsuccessful German offensive towards Budapest. A special railway truck had to be provided to transport it from one part of the front to another.

Russian Grenadier (1814)

military figures, thanks to the literature and paintings which have made him famous.

Drummer boys were very young boys who joined the army at only twelve years of age to take up a career as non-commissioned officers. They did not carry arms but were regarded as real soldiers.

It was their duty to beat the drums not only as part of the band during military parades but also during battle or at special moments when the fighting was at its fiercest. Drums were used to give the signal to break camp, advance and retreat.

The drum beats provided a rallying point and gave the soldiers a sense of community and safety. This is essential when men are fighting for their lives.

Why rifle ammunition is called cartridges

Until the middle of the nineteenth century, when you wanted to fire a rifle, you had to prepare the firing device, compress the explosive charge in order to get a more powerful explosion, and then place the bullet in close contact with the powder.

All this obviously took a long time and as the years passed improved systems were developed to permit much faster loading of the weapon.

The explosive charge, the priming device and the bullet were finally combined into a single paper holder, or cartouche, so as to be ready for use.

From this primitive wrapping is derived the name of the modern cartridge, which is made of cardboard, metal or plastic.

filled with gunpowder which, when ignited, caused an explosion. Heavy balls were thrown to varying distances, depending on the length of the barrel and the size of the explosive charge.

For about 600 years gun powder was the only explosive; then, in the middle of the nineteenth century, nitroglycerin and nitrocellulose were discovered.

Why every army had drummer boys

The drummer boy is without any doubt one of the best known

Why we speak of war of movement and trench warfare

The First World War (1914–18) seemed as though it should have been characterized by great troop movements, especially on the western front, that is the line between France and Germany. It was thought that with the tremendous build-up of powerful weapons, especially artillery, on both sides, the front would crumble resulting in a subsequent massive advance.

In actual fact, this rarely happened. The balance of forces in the field and the nature of the terrain brought about the so-called trench warfare.

On both sides of the front for kilometres, long trenches were dug in which soldiers of the opposing armies faced one another and fought continually but only succeeded in changing the original lines very slightly.

This situation went on for months and then years without any definite result on either side other than the deteriorating condition of the troops.

Why uniforms were once brightly coloured

The uniforms worn by modern soldiers are usually very drab or even camouflaged. In battle some special corps wear uniforms which are adapted to their surroundings; for instance, in a snow-covered area white uniforms are essential.

At one time the need to camouflage the combatants, that is to make them less visible to the enemy, was not considered an important factor. There were many reasons why uniforms were almost always in bright colours, but the basic need was to be able to distinguish the different regiments, friend or foe.

It was necessary to recognize the enemy at once in furious hand to hand fighting. In particular the supreme commander, usually stationed on a height overlooking the field of battle, had to pick out his own troops and take in the general situation at a glance.

Today brightly coloured uniforms are normally reserved for ceremonial occasions when the emphasis is on pageantry and splendour.

Rocket launching Typhoons attack German armoured vehicles

Why barbed wire was used in the First World War

There is one thing which often occurs in literature and painting as a symbol of the war fought in the trenches, and that is barbed wire.

These entanglements were made of kilometre upon kilometre of barbed wire, all intertwined and supported on special iron stakes. They were set up in front of the trenches along the whole length to impede the advance of the enemy.

At a time when tanks were in their infancy and hand to hand fighting was still the rule, barbed wire often proved to be an impassable barrier. It was so closely interwoven that it was often impossible to get rid of it even by massive artillery action. The small gaps which were sometimes opened up during the fighting could usually be closed again in a very short time.

The defence behind the lines of barbed wire was made even more effective by the deadly fire of machine guns.

Why the Japanese used kamikaze

A piloted rocket bomb

During the Second World War the Japanese gave the task of attacking and destroying the enemy ships to their air force. The air force was supplied with fast planes and a large number of volunteer airmen prepared to die in the attempt; anyone who became a kamikaze renounced any chance of returning alive.

The word 'kamikaze' means 'divine wind' and was given to this undertaking to indicate that those taking part would make the supreme sacrifice in the name of their divine emperor and destroy the enemy.

The kamikaze planes, laden with powerful explosives and piloted by young men filled with the spirit of self-sacrifice, dived down on to the enemy vessels by the score, causing serious damage.

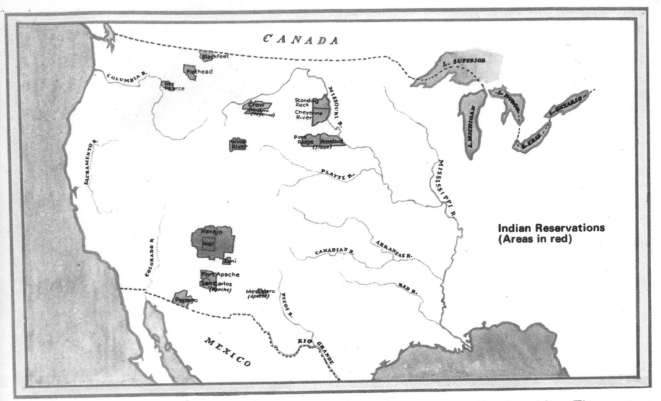

Indian Reservations
(Areas in red)

Why the first American settlers exterminated the redskins

The American government had on many occasions promised the various Indian tribes that they would respect certain territories which would remain areas reserved for the redskins only. These agreements, however, were never respected by the whites. The greatest enemies of the Indians were those who, through need or greed, were driven to occupy those enormous tracts of uncultivated land which promised such rich harvests.

From this arose the interminable conflicts which went on for years and affected many innocent victims on both sides.

Why the Indians now live in reserves

Why the United States are so called

The Signing of the Declaration of Independence, 4 July 1776

It was a black future that was reserved for the descendants of the Indians. The ever advancing waves of the white conquerors demanded more and more space; there could be no place for anyone who left unproductive huge areas of land as big as whole states. The Indians were to be guaranteed their liberty but in a very much reduced territory.

To a very great extent those who had ruled over immense hunting grounds and were forced without hope into small reserves, refused to mix with the white population and preferred to lead a very impoverished life in order to keep their integrity as a nation.

Almost a century has now passed since the decline of the redskins but they still retain the traditions, costumes and rites of their ancestors. They live mainly by their own work as artisans, peasants and tourist attractions.

In 1775 the first conflicts arose between the English settlers in America and the government at home. On 10 June 1776 the so-called Articles of Union were approved; these were the first attempt by the English colonies in America to draw up a constitution of self government.

The Declaration of Independence was approved on 4 July 1776. This act of total rebellion against the mother country was the beginning of war between the English and the new citizens of the Union. They belonged to thirteen colonies which from that moment became independent states but united among themselves in a federation. The Federal Constitution had to be accepted by nine out of thirteen states. On 21 June 1788 the ninth state ratified the Constitution and on 4 March 1789 the United States of America was born.

Why Venice became wealthy as a result of the Crusades

The geographical position of Venice, its magnificent fleet and the political ability of its rulers

were all factors of great importance in a situation such as that created by the Crusades. The First Crusade had shown that to reach the Holy Land by the overland route was a long undertaking beset with many snares. To transport the troops by sea meant a saving of valuable time and a much safer journey.

But transport costs money and the Republic of Venice charged very high prices for the services it supplied. As a result the Crusades became a real gold mine for the Venetians who took advantage of these journeys of the Crusaders to increase their own business.

The greatest profits were made by Venice when she did not ask for payment in money but in help. It happened during the Fourth Crusade (1202–4); the organizers did not have the means of transporting the troops and Venice offered her services in return for a favour, military help against the city of Zara which had rebelled against Venice. The Crusaders kept their promise but Venice raised the price and asked for further military help to put a trusted friend, Isaac d'Angelo, on the throne of Constantinople. This caused a whole series of complications which all turned out to be very profitable for the Venetians. They occupied the main islands of the Aegean and ensured for themselves control of the Bosphorus and the Dardanelles.

Why flags were invented

The story of flags started at sea. From very remote times navigators needed to signal their identity both to people on land and also to the vessels they met at sea. In addition during the Crusades it became necessary to distinguish the combatants and that is why many modern flags originated under such circumstances. A clear indication of this is that the cross is still frequently included in the flags of many nations.

For purposes of signalling and identification flags must fly out in the wind, so they are usually made of a light material with an indentical pattern on both sides.

Why the power of Spain declined in 1588

Spain's period of greatest splendour was in the time of the Emperor Charles V (1500–58). Her predominance in Europe was reinforced by the great wealth brought back from the New World.

There was only one power which stood in the way of that supremacy, England. Philip II, the son of Charles V, tried to put down the competition of this rival by an expedition consisting of more than 130 warships. Even before it had engaged in a single battle it was called the Invincible Armada.

The most decisive encounter took place on 8 August 1588 off the coast of Gravelines, in France, and ended in the total defeat of the Spaniards.

Perhaps never before, as in this case, had a single military defeat brought about the overthrow of a great power; the countries subject to Spain began to raise their heads and the supremacy at sea passed unquestionably to the English.

Why tanks were built

The idea of using a kind of moving and powerfully armed fortress occurred during the period before the First World War. The first tanks in the modern sense of the word were the English ones which went into action during the battle of the Somme in September 1916. This type of self-propelled armoured vehicle was given the name tank because of its box-like appearance. In the Second World War tanks were developed to an extraordinary extent: they were provided with armour plate to withstand enemy shells and fitted with bigger and better guns.

Despite the invention of powerful anti-tank weapons, the tank still maintains its original features: mobility (up to 80 kilometres an hour) and power of attack.

Why submarines were used so much in the Second World War

In the two World Wars Germany was in conflict with Great Britain which obtained regular supplies of food and arms by sea from the Commonwealth and the United States. Germany therefore carried out special naval operations aimed at sinking as many British and Allied ships as possible.

In the First World War one form which this took was the use of sea-raiders, mainly surface vessels, which the Germans used with great skill and ability. They met with a certain degree of limited success.

In the Second World War the Germans concentrated more on the use of their U-boats or submarines. From August 1940 to May 1943 they waged furious war against Allied convoys in the North Atlantic and sank hundreds of ships. During these three years of sea warfare the U-boats made use of several forms of attack, the final one being by packs of U-boats which combined to attack our convoys.

Why aircraft carriers were built

Many people realized after the First World War that the decisive weapon of the future would be the aeroplane.

Not everyone, however, understood that the air force would have to operate with the navy as well as with the other branches of the armed services.

The countries which were convinced of this need, and in particular the United States and Japan, built ships fitted out specially for the purpose and they were called aircraft carriers.

There were many advantages to be gained by this, two in particular: effective air cover was provided for ships and convoys and by this means air bases could be established in any place required by the progress of the war.

Modern aircraft carriers are colossal ships, often powered by nuclear engines, able to carry scores of fighter aircraft and helicopters. Many have a ramp at one end of the runway to help thrust the aircraft into the air as they take off.

The V2 rocket, the largest and most advanced missile of the Second World War

The V1 flying bomb: its low speed (620 kph) made it very vulnerable

called them *Vergeltungswaffen* (reprisal weapons) and they were therefore known by the letter 'V'.

The VI was a kind of unmanned aeroplane which was intended to fall on predetermined targets. In September 1944, three months after the V1, which was faulty and not very fast, the Germans were able to launch the V2. This rocket reached a speed of 5,600 kilometres an hour and carried a warhead of about a ton of explosive.

London was the main target of both the V1 and the V2 and many lives were lost and much damage caused by them.

Why the V1 and V2 were such deadly weapons

The need to launch deadly contrivances at a distance has always been one of man's basic problems in war.

During the last World War when Germany had definitely lost the air supremacy, the Germans devised new weapons to launch very explosive projectiles over long distances. These weapons were based on the principal of rocket propulsion. The Germans

The British aircraft carrier *Ark Royal* (1946)

THE WHY OF GEOGRAPHY

Why maps have the north at the top

Ancient cartographers always regarded Ptolemy as the master map maker. He was an Egyptian scientist who had produced the best maps known in the ancient world 150 years after Christ. Ptolemy drew in the centre of his map the part of the world which he considered the most important, Egypt. To the north of Egypt were the Mediterranean Basin and Greece, with which Egypt had frequent contact, and Ptolemy therefore marked the north at the top of his map. Since then all map makers have done the same.

There is, therefore, no exact scientific basis for the origin of this common setting of maps. Indeed in the Middle Ages when the generals taking part in the Crusades and the merchants dealing in spices had to travel eastwards, maps were drawn with the east at the top and the north on the left.

From tne practical point of view one system is as good as the other. What matters is that the cardinal points on the map should be indicated in such a way that countries which are really situated to the north of the countries shown in the centre of the map appear to the north on the map, and those which lie to the south are shown to the south of the centre on the map, and so on.

Why we talk about getting our bearings

Suppose that we are about to make a long journey in an unknown and deserted country where there are neither streets nor signposts. What would we do to keep in mind the itinerary we are following and to record the route to follow on the way back? We would look carefully around and try to fix in our memory some specific unmistakable details of the way: curiously shaped rocks, hills, a group of trees, and so on. On our return, when we come to these landmarks we shall know that we are on the right path.

But suppose that we have to travel across the desert or the immense steppes or the sea, what landmarks have we? This was the first problem which had to be solved by the early travellers when they ventured into unknown lands or the open sea. As they had no points of reference on the land they turned their attention to the sky.

They had noticed that the Sun appeared to rise and set at the same places on the horizon. Where the Sun rose they called east and where it set they called west and decided to take the east as their point of reference for their travels. That is why we talk about getting our bearings or orientation, from the word 'orient' which means east.

Why the Pole Star is important

On a clear night it is possible to find the north by looking at the sky. There is one star which always remains in the same place and the others seem to revolve around it. This is the Pole Star which sailors recognize easily; it shows where the north is and from it all the other points of the compass can then be worked out. It is also used in determining latitude.

Although the Pole Star appears to be a single star to the naked eye, it is really a group of three stars.

South of the equator where the Pole Star is not visible we can find our bearings by the Southern Cross, a constellation which indicates the direction of the South Pole.

Why we use the cardinal points

In order to work out correctly which way to go on a journey or the direction of a place, a single point of reference such as where the Sun rises or sets is not enough. For this reason the ancients agreed to fix four basic or cardinal points to which reference could be made.

These points are north, south, east and west. If we know where the east is it is easy to discover the other cardinal points: all you have to do is to stand facing the place where the Sun rises: the north will then be on your left hand, the south on your right and the west, where the Sun sets, will be behind you.

For giving intermediate directions between the four cardinal points, we use the points of the compass.

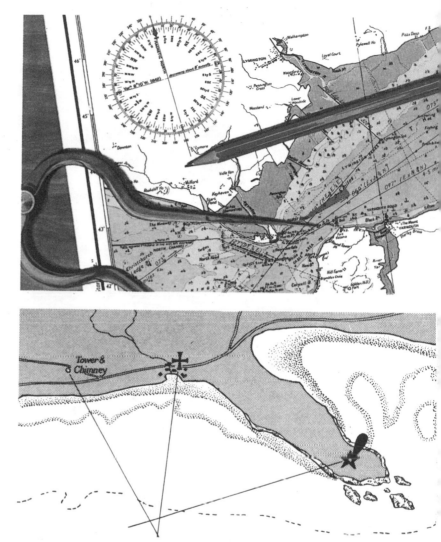

To fix the exact direction for a journey reference is made to the cardinal points fixed by the ancients

Why the climate is always mild along the coast

The seas, and to some extent the lakes as well, act like storage

heaters and tend to equalize the climate. During the day when the rays of the Sun beat down on the Earth the sea stores up heat, but very slowly because water has a lower power of absorbing heat than the rocks and sand.

However, just as it is slow to heat up, it is also slow to cool down again. During the night when the soil of the shore and of the surrounding land tends to lose quickly the heat received from the Sun, the water releases it little by little, keeping the air mild until the following morning. This explains why on the sea coast there are no great leaps in temperature between day and night.

However, if we look at this over the four seasons of the year we see that from spring to summer the sea water warms up very slowly and even in the heat of summer it is never as hot as the sand or as the air at sea level. Therefore as it comes into contact with the air it helps to mitigate the heat and make the climate of the coast bearable even on the hottest summer day. When we add to this the factor of evaporation which is a powerful one, although invisible, and also lowers the temperature, we can realize why it is so pleasant at the seaside in the summer.

When the cold season comes, the position is reversed: from October onwards the sea shore cools very quickly whereas the sea releases its store of heat only gradually and therefore keeps the climate mild even in winter.

Why there are warm regions and cold regions

Because the Earth is a sphere the rays of the Sun reach the surface at different angles: at the equator they are almost perpendicular and therefore pass through a thinner layer of atmosphere, there is less absorption by atmospheric dust and they are hotter. At the Poles the reverse is the case.

As a result it is possible to define various zones north and south of the equator with different characteristics of climate determined precisely by the angle at which the Sun's rays reach the surface.

Scientists have agreed to divide the Earth into five areas: two frigid zones, the north and south polar regions; two temperate zones between the polar regions and the tropics, and one torrid zone along the equator.

The winds, the sea, and the presence of hot or cold currents also effect the temperature of an area.

Why some plants can live even in the desert

The areas of the Earth which have the richest vegetation are those immediately to the north and south of the equator. This is in fact the region where, as a result of intense evaporation, the greatest concentration of clouds occurs. These give rise to torrential rains which combined with the heat favour the growth of vegetation.

But in those places, such as the deserts, where the complex play of the winds does not allow the clouds to accumulate, it does not mean that the ground is completely without moisture. Occasional showers of rain fall although sometimes years may elapse between them. It would seem impossible for any form of vegetable life to exist under such conditions: there are, nevertheless, some plants which manage to grow and increase here because of special features which enable them to overcome the lack of moisture. They are known as xerophilous plants, that is plants which like dry conditions.

The largest group of these plants is that of the cacti which are to be found particularly in the tropical regions of America and also in Africa and Madagascar. These plants have no leaves and this eliminates to a very large extent the transpiration which usually takes place through the leaves.

Chlorophyll function occurs through the trunks which are green in colour because of the presence of chlorophyll in their epidermis. They are usually spherical or cylindrical in shape and provide an excellent reservoir which fills with water whenever it does rain.

Why houses vary in style from one region to another

Ever since man first moved out of the caves he has built himself some kind of shelter in which to take refuge during the night and in bad weather.

Even when men changed from a nomadic and wandering life and began to spend a large part of their time in their dwellings, their houses were still built for the purpose of providing a roof and a shelter.

All those features which have been added in later periods and have led to the development of different styles of architecture peculiar to each region, depend very much on the resources of the place in which men chose to live.

That is why the winter dwellings of the Eskimos are made with blocks of ice, which is the only material available in these desolate Arctic regions.

Likewise on the steppes of Russia the huts were built mostly of wood which was plentiful in those parts. On the plains of Africa which are rich in tall grass the dwellings are made of a mixture of straw and mud.

For the same reason the ancient monuments of Mesopotamia were built of clay bricks because in that alluvial region it was impossible to find rocks, whereas in mountainous areas the walls and even the roofs are made of stone.

Each type of material imposed its own particular technique of building and shape of dwelling and from this arose the different styles.

The tower-keep of Hirosaki Castle in Japan

Why roofs in mountainous areas are very steep

The surroundings and in particular the climate have a very great influence on human dwellings. For instance, in very sunny places windows are usually small and those most exposed to the Sun have verandas in order to create areas of shade. In northern regions, however, where sunshine and light are scarce the houses have large windows and glass doors. Where it rains little, as in tropical countries, there is no need for sloping roofs and therefore the roofs of the houses tend to be made into terraces. On the other hand where there is a greater degree of rain the roof must be strong and with a good slope. When a house is built in the mountains the roof has to be able to bear the weight of the snow in winter and this can be quite considerable. To prevent successive falls of snow from bearing too heavily on it, the roof is made with a very steep slope so that beyond a certain limit the snow slides off it to the ground.

Why they build skyscrapers

The growth of towns is a feature of our times. Very many people are leaving the country and villages and moving into the towns attracted by the mirage of a more comfortable and glamorous life and increased chances of wealth and success. Towns and cities are growing to bursting point whilst the rural populations are becoming smaller and smaller.

To provide for all these people more houses are needed in the towns. As the demand grows so the prices of houses continually increase, and building land in the cities becomes scarce and very expensive. This also contributes to the high cost of living accommodation.

If there is not enough space to build houses of the traditional type, what is to be done? They build houses one on top of another and use the same land for several families. That is how the idea of skyscrapers came about: multi-storey buildings result in a saving of land, which it is now almost impossible to find in the cities.

The idea of skyscrapers is not new to this century. It had already been adopted by the ancients; for

The banks of the River Niger

instance, the Romans used to build large blocks of flats which they called *insulae* and which housed many of the poorer families. But their buildings could not go beyond a certain height because they lacked suitable building materials and also because by means of stairs alone it was quite a task to climb to the higher floors.

Modern skyscrapers only became possible with the invention of lifts and the use of new materials such as steel and reinforced concrete.

Why clouds do not always mean rain

At every moment of the day and night large amounts of water vapour are drawn up from the surface of the Earth in tiny invisible drops. The water of the seas, lakes and rivers is constantly being evaporated. When we hang out our washing on the line we find after some time that it is dry, which means that the water it contained has passed into the air. Incredible amounts of water in the form of vapour are given off by plants as part of their chemical activity in the production of organic substances.

Where does all this water vapour go to?

The answer is into the sky: it rises moment by moment, higher and higher because it is lighter than air. But when it reaches the cold levels of the atmosphere the vapour condenses, the drops of water combine and the vapour becomes visible as clouds, which are nothing more than masses of water vapour which have reached a certain stage of condensation. Wind and air currents then take control of the clouds and drive them all in a given direction, but at this stage the water vapour, although dense, still remains lighter than air, and therefore there is no rainfall.

Rain occurs when there is excessive concentration of vapour due to the action of the wind or to a further fall in temperature which causes the drops of vapour to condense still more to form heavy drops which can no longer be supported by the air. At this point they begin to fall back on to the surface of the Earth in the form of rain.

cirrus   cirro-stratus

Why lightning occurs during thunderstorms

Lightning is a sudden violent discharge of electricity from cloud to cloud or from cloud to Earth under certain conditions. It is, on a much larger scale, the same phenomenon which can be seen if the positive and negative terminals of a car battery are accidentally connected together to form a short circuit. The sudden dazzling flash of short duration which we see in this case is of the same nature as lightning. The same thing happens between cloud masses of opposite electric charges or with a single cloud mass where the positive and negative charges have collected at opposite ends, or between clouds and Earth.

In all these cases we have lightning, which is a rapid succession of discharges, each lasting about 500 microseconds. Because each discharge takes place at a definite point along the line of least electrical resistance we have the optical illusion that it is a single flash of lightning which travels at high speed across the sky or down to Earth.

alto-stratus   *nimbo-stratus*

Why there are low clouds and high clouds

When we know the nature and mechanism of cloud formation we can also explain why clouds are able to float lower or higher in the sky.

Although these large masses of concentrated water vapour are at the mercy of the winds, their existence depends above all upon the atmospheric conditions around them.

If the air is quite warm up to a great altitude the vapour can rise to exceptional heights without cooling to the point of changing into rain.

On the other hand, if currents of cold air pass over a region at a relatively low level the vapour will condense when it meets them and will not rise any further.

Atmospheric pressure also plays a large part in this process and whether clouds rise to higher or lower levels depends upon the complex balance between air temperature, pressure, the degree of condensation and the specific gravity of the vapour.

Why there is fog in winter

In humid places early in the morning and towards evening the water vapour condenses around the fine dust in the atmosphere near to the ground to form fog, the density of which depends upon the season of the year and the temperature. Fog is white in the country but in towns it is grey and soot-laden.

In some regions where there are certain geographical conditions (lack of wind, particular atmospheric pressures) the fog stays near the ground for several months of the year in the bad season and makes it difficult for people and traffic to get about.

When this process takes place over large industrial cities the fog mixes with the soot and smoke from industrial and domestic chimneys and becomes smog, which is very harmful to both people and materials.

All in all fog can be regarded as a cloud which remains close to the ground instead of rising into the upper layers of the atmosphere. Artificial ways of dispersing it are being investigated.

Why sea breezes change direction morning and evening

Among regular winds the commonest are the sea and land breezes. These are very light local winds caused by the difference of temperature between land and sea.

Formation of a cold valley wind (above) and a warm mountain wind (below)

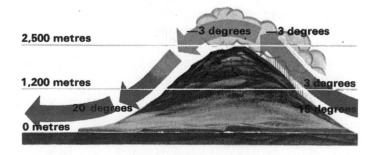

During the day the earth warms up more quickly than the sea and therefore the air above it becomes lighter and rises, creating an area of rarefied atmosphere at ground level. The air above the sea, which is colder and therefore more compressed and heavier, is drawn into this area. This causes a wind from the sea to blow towards the land, that is a sea breeze.

Towards evening and during the night, on the other hand, the wind changes direction and goes from the land to the sea, that is a land breeze. This happens because the land cools more easily and brings about a similar cooling of the air which therefore moves to replace the air above the sea which now remains warm. This is well known to all fishermen who time their departure by it. Nowadays when boats use engines and are no longer dependent on the wind it is no more than a pleasant feature of coastal areas.

Why there are winds

Atmospheric pressure, that is the weight of the air above the Earth, is subject to continual variations. Like all gases the air increases in volume as the temperature rises, which means that a cubic metre of cold air weighs more than a cubic metre of hot air.

The air moves from the cold regions of the Earth where the air is heavier to the warm regions and displaces the lighter air there which tends to rise and cause rarefied zones in the lower levels of the atmosphere. It is this displacement which causes winds.

A wind therefore is a horizontal displacement of air from a high pressure area to a low pressure one and vice-versa. The wind varies in strength according to the difference in pressure between the two areas.

Winds can be classified as periodic, constant, local and cyclonic. Constant winds are those which blow in the same direction all the year round as can be seen over the oceans when there are no disturbing influences. Local winds are those which only affect small areas. Periodic winds are those which blow in one direction at one time and in the opposite direction at another time.

Why cyclones occur

Cyclonic winds are exceptionally violent movements of air masses. They blow mostly from the tropics where areas of hot air are formed. The surrounding colder air flows towards them with a whirling movement which spirals upwards or spreads out horizontally.

The atmospheric disturbance which they cause is called a cyclone. Cyclones blow from west to east and often cause extensive damage in the areas over which they pass. They also change the pattern of atmospheric precipitation all around. For this reason they are carefully studied and tracked in their movements, even with the use of special weather planes. These can penetrate into the eye of the cyclone, that is the centre of the enormous and turbulent vortex of clouds, where the air is very quiet and they are therefore able to study the conditions without being tossed dangerously about by the wind.

Weather maps show that there are relatively permanent cyclonic centres in the northern Atlantic and Pacific oceans.

Why tornados occur

During a hurricane or cyclone it can happen that vortices of air are formed at some points and although they are not very extensive they are very fast.

In certain conditions two whirlwinds of air, one on the ground and the other in the sky, may meet and touch one another with opposite points, like two cones one on top of the other with the points in contact. The two frightful forms then unite and, revolving tumultuously with a speed of rotation of as much as 200 kilometres an hour, move in the dominant direction of the wind.

The speed at which a tornado moves is not very high, about 60 kilometres an hour, and the diameter of the vortex is only a few hundred metres at the most.

Tornados carry away objects, root up trees and houses and often cause the death of people and animals (above right). Waterspouts (bottom right) cause less damage because they can more easily be anticipated.
Enormous damage is, however, caused by sandstorms (below). The fine grains of sand penetrate everywhere and damage machinery and equipment over a wide area through their abrasive action.

Why the sea sometimes rises and floods large areas of land

Because of the complex state of equilibrium of the surface strata of the Earth's crust there is in many places, right beneath our feet, a constant rising or falling of the ground which occurs century after century, but it is so slow as to be imperceptible to our normal senses'.

This phenomenon, which causes slow, vertical movements of the Earth's crust, is evident on the coast. Here it is possible to see whether a rocky coast was once higher or lower in relation to the sea level than it is at the present time because traces of erosion still remain.

If we see a rock with signs of erosion by the waves at a height of 15 or 20 metres, we can deduce that at one time it was 15 or 20 metres lower, otherwise how could we explain this hammering by the waves at that height?

If, then, this phenomenon takes place on low lying coasts the land which sinks is covered by the sea advancing over quite a long distance; or vast areas rise and then it is the sea which retreats little by little leaving behind the uncovered land.

Sometimes these movements alternate: that is to say that for centuries the land continues to rise and then begins to sink once again.

Evidence of this is to be found at Puzzuoli, an ancient seaside town in southern Italy. The volcanic qualities of the area have resulted in hot springs and changes in the level of land. Buildings have been submerged by the sea. An example of this is the temple of Serapis, which was certainly built on firm ground far from the sea. Then the land sank, the sea was able to advance and the temple was submerged up to a certain height. Later the land rose again but the columns still retain traces of erosion and of some small marine animals.

Fifty years ago the temple was entirely on dry land but today it has again begun to sink.

A column from the temple of Serapis at Pozzuoli

Why waves form on the sea

There are many kinds of waves both on the surface and inside the sea. They are caused by the wind blowing over the sea, by underwater earthquakes and by the effects of the Sun and Moon. The last are called astronomical tides.

If we blow across a basin full of water we can see at once the way in which waves are formed by the wind. It blows over the surface of the sea, making the waves large or small according to its force and intensity.

But the wind does not cause any movement of the water from one place to another, or drive it in any one direction; even when it forms very high waves the water remains practically still.

That is to say that the waves are the rise and fall of the individual drops of water on the surface of the sea; they make a closed circular movement in a vertical direction.

The movement spreads and therefore the waves seem to chase one another as far as the eye can see.

Why there is sand on the beach

Beaches are the dumping grounds of the seas. For millions of years the winds and the tides have beaten day and night against the rocky coasts, hammering, shaking and bombarding them with fragments.

Under these blows the rocks very gradually crack, split, crumble and are reduced to minute grains. This is how sand is made as a result of the continuous struggle between the sea and the rocks. The waves then carry off the

very fine particles of rock and the ocean currents take them far away.

In the quieter inlets along low lying coasts the waters of the sea calm down and allow the sand they are carrying to fall onto the bottom. In the course of time this accumulates into large deposits and the waves spread it out gently on the shore to form the beach.

Not all the sand comes from the rocks which the sea wears away along the high coasts; a very large proportion of the sand is brought to the sea by the rivers which carry it down from the mountains.

Why icebergs are found in Arctic seas

All glaciers move, although with extreme slowness like huge solid rivers.

Likewise the immense glaciers which cover the northern regions move and descend slowly towards the sea. They are sometimes hundreds of metres thick and together they present above the surface of the sea a vast front like a range of mountain peaks.

The exact volume of glaciers is not known but it has been estimated that there is enough ice to encase the entire Earth in a layer between 30 and 60 metres thick.

Glaciers cannot stop moving because of the immense pressure of the continuous masses of ice behind them. They therefore slide on towards the sea, advancing all the time until, when there is emptiness beneath them, they break up into blocks which break loose and float on the sea at the mercy of the currents.

Icebergs, as these floating mountains of ice are called, are particularly common on the coast of Greenland, from where they continue along the North American coast. When they reach the Newfoundland Banks most of them come into the region of a warm current and melt, nearly always at the same place.

The famous Banks were in fact formed by the accumulation of enormous quantities of rocks and mud carried inside the icebergs and then deposited on the bottom of the sea as the icebergs melt.

Why the Vikings gave Greenland its name

Some 55 million years ago in the Eocene Period (the second period of the Tertiary Era) the climate on Earth was uniformly temperate and made it possible for life to develop far to the north, even beyond the Arctic Circle.

Flowering plants were then spread everywhere as a result of the activity of bees and other pollinating insects, thus ensuring their reproduction.

But their geographical distribution was quite different. Because of its favourable climate Greenland was covered with forests of palms and other vegetation which are now to be found only in the tropical zones. As time went on, however, the climate changed; it became much colder in the north and distribution of living creatures also changed.

Eric the Red called the land Greenland in 985, probably to encourage more people to go there with him.

Why the great glaciations are not yet finished

After the first great glaciation which began about a million years ago and lasted for some 100,000 years the temperature on Earth became milder and the glaciers retreated northwards, but only for a short time.

The great cold returned four times and four times the ice retreated, leaving enormous moraine deposits in its path.

The last great retreat of the ice began more than 10,000 years ago and still continues today. Studies which were made during the international geophysical year have, in fact, shown that the ice at the poles is still decreasing and the level of the oceans is rising.

During the glacial periods mammals of giant size such as the mastodon and some ferocious carnivores developed, and among the fossil remains of these animals traces of the first men have also been found.

Why glaciers wear away the rocks

There are three ways in which glaciers contribute to the erosion and breakdown of the rocks: by scraping away the bottom of glacial valleys like powerful rasps, by wearing away pieces of the overhanging rocks and by carrying down with them the rocks which fall on to them.

The first erosive action is due to the fact that glaciers are always moving downwards and therefore scrape slowly over the rocks beneath. It is true that the ice is not as hard as the rocks and is not able to scratch them, but many pebbles and sometimes even large

stones pass through the crevasses to the bottom of the glacier in contact with the ground.

Through the movement of the glacier these pebbles and stones scrape heavily upon the rocks below wearing away small pieces, which then reinforce the rasping action of the glacier. This is the reason why old glacial valleys have very smooth walls, sometimes with deep horizontal grooves.

Glaciers act indirectly on the rock walls above them: during the day the rocks exposed to the Sun warm up and expand, but during the night they cool down again because of the cold induced by the nearness of the glacier, and the surface of the rocks contracts.

In the long run these variations of volume cause the rocks to disintegrate and the pieces to fall on to the glacier which then carries them along with it.

Why the Great Barrier Reef was formed

The Great Barrier Reef which extends for thousands of kilometres along the north-east coast of Australia from Torres strait to beyond the tropic of Capricorn, is the most famous coral formation in the world. It is like an enormous wall erected between the sea and the land, and is formed of a very high layer of coral composed of the accumulation of coral skeletons. By their unceasing activity over

with no thin ramifications which would be broken.

On the other side where the barrier reef itself creates an area of calm sea, the colonies of polyps make a diversity of shapes, flowers, shrubs and bone-lace which create a dream landscape.

The spaces between one colony and another are filled with coral fragments broken down by the sea and forming a fertile sludge.

On this limestone soil brought down by the waves, numerous algae grow and many marine

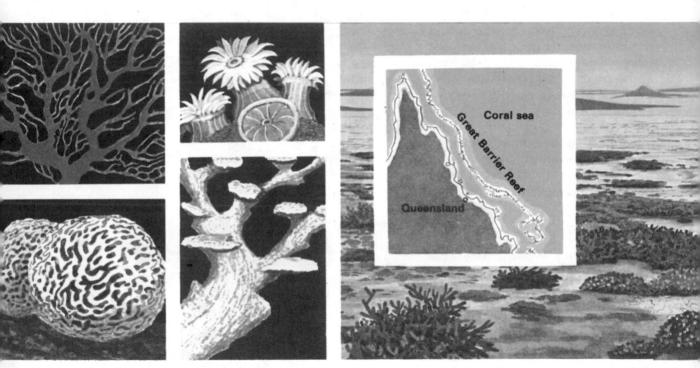

millions of years these polyps have built complete islands of coral rock in the open oceans.

In these warm, tropical seas the water is rich in food, the light of the Sun is strong and the coral colonies prosper and produce brightly coloured, fantastic shapes.

Towards the open sea where the waves beat violently on the reef the layers of coral are compact

animals flourish with their vivid colours and curious shapes. Shoals of fish pass by the brilliant expanses of coral and disappear into the darkness.

Typical inhabitants of the coral reefs are the butterfly fish, small and brightly coloured, which nose among the crevices of coral in search of food.

Why there are tides

Tides are periodical fluctuations of the sea which occur twice a day. When the water is high we call it high tide and when the water is low it is low tide. Naturally the rising level of the sea leads to a horizontal movement on the low-lying coasts and the water covers large areas of sand; at low tide the beach becomes dry once more.

The extent of the tides is not always the same and equal in all parts of the world. It is very strong at the new Moon and the full Moon because tides are caused by the attraction of the Moon, which at those periods is added to that of the Sun. It is also more accentuated in the open seas.

It would not be correct, however, to imagine that the Moon acts like a huge magnet and draws towards it the seas which come under its influence. The nature of this attraction is much more complex because the effect of the Moon interferes with the effects of the Earth's gravity and the centrifugal force due to the speed of rotation of the Earth.

Why some islands are ring-shaped

Ring-shaped islands, called atolls, are very common in the Pacific Ocean. They are formed of millions of coral shells piled on one another and cemented together.

In the warm seas these colonies of tiny animals flourish in huge numbers and build picturesque layers of coral shells in the most varied shapes. When the coral polyps attach themselves to the coasts of a small submerged island, they gradually build all around it a ring of coral which increases in size.

The island continues to sink and is submerged to a considerable depth: all around on the surface of the water is a large ring of coral colonies which go on developing. At a certain point the island may begin to rise again and lift up with it the ring of coral until it is above the water level. The wind and the waves then carry on to it the first seeds and the atoll is covered with vegetation.

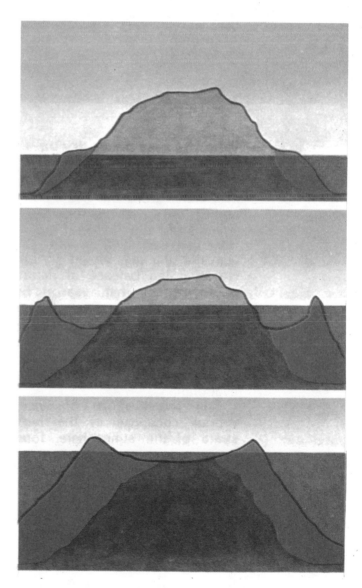

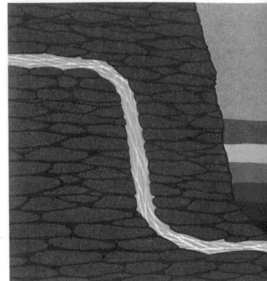

Why the seas never dry up

The amount of water which evaporates from the sea in the course of a year is enormous: millions of cubic metres. Eventually, therefore, you would expect that the seas would dry up. However the balance of nature is so perfect that, season by season, all the water which was drawn up into the skies returns in various ways to the seas. That is why the level of the seas can remain constantly the same despite evaporation.

The tiniest drops of water vapour condense in the high strata of the atmosphere, form into clouds and return to Earth as rain, snow and sleet. If they fall on the sea the balance is restored at once. On the other hand if they fall on the land they go to feed the springs and streams which carry them back to the sea. This cycle of water continues for ever.

So long as it continues to meet porous material such as gravel, sand and limestone, rain water sinks deeper into the ground, but when it meets a layer of impermeable rock or clay it is forced to stop. The water then spreads out and saturates all the ground above the impermeable layer and at the same time seeks a way out. In this state the subterranean water can be reached by wells from which it can be pumped up to the surface.

But the sheet of water contained in the porous material may find itself imprisoned between two layers of impermeable rocks at an angle or in the form of a basin. The water is then almost as if in a pressure pipe and its pressure is greater than atmospheric pressure. If we bore into the ground, that is open up a way out for it, the water will rise spontaneously to the surface, often gushing to a height. Wells of this type are called artesian wells.

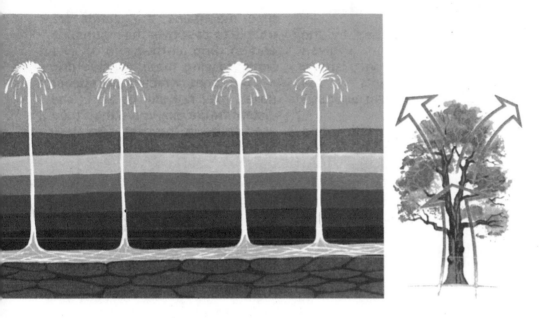

The water cycle (left); artesian wells (bottom left); water also evaporates through plants and returns into the cycle once again (bottom right).

Why even large rivers have several tributaries

At its source even the greatest river is only a small stream or tiny waterfall of little importance. If it were not enriched by other water along its course it would never even manage to reach the sea.

A watercourse can have a definite origin such as a spring or the region of a glacier, but most often it is formed from rain water or the melting of snows, the water of which runs down in rivulets and collects into one bed.

Watercourses are generally divided into streams and rivers, but it would be more correct to say that streams are simply early forms of watercourses which run down and are swollen by the water from tributaries and thus become rivers.

A watercourse can be regarded as a river when it flows slowly over almost level plains and its volume of water is quite regular.

In the plains the watercourses flow towards the sea at a speed which is related to the height of their source: the lower the source, the slower the speed. As the water no longer has the impetuous force which it possessed in the mountain valleys, it cannot scoop out for itself a straight path in the plain and therefore every small obstacle (harder ground, rocky projections and even merely tangles of roots) may force the river to change direction.

As a result the course of the river becomes winding and it sometimes meanders across the plain. At this stage the river gives up finer detritus and deposits it on the river bed and on the banks in the form of a very fine mud.

Why some regions are desert

By desert we mean an area where it rains very little and at long, irregular intervals.

Rainfall is determined by the massing of clouds in a given region, and so what is very largely responsible for deserts is the wind which fails to bring clouds to some areas.

If we look at a map of the world we shall see that almost all the deserts are concentrated in a band about 20° latitude north and south: just those areas known for their stable high pressures where the conditions never arise for the formation of cloud systems.

Another reason for the formation of deserts is the great distance of some areas from the sea. The cloud systems which come from the oceans discharge their rain on the way and have no water left when they reach these regions. For the same reason deserts can occur at the foot of high mountains: the clouds are unable to pass over the mountains and so drop all their rain on one slope, leaving the other side dry.

The zones which now appear desert may not still be so in the distant future, any more than they used to be in the past. The slow rate of change is due precisely to the characteristics of a desert region. If the ground were covered with dense vegetation the moisture in the soil would be protected from the rays of the Sun and evaporation would be much reduced. Modern techniques of dry cultivation may make it an economical proposition to apply this process of a covering of vegetation, which is the only way to ensure the definite recovery of vast areas of the Earth which are at the moment sterile.

Why embankments are built along rivers

Floods generally occur when there is a thaw and it is difficult to forecast when this will happen.

For this reason the banks of the large rivers are reinforced by powerful embankments calculated to withstand any increase that may occur during the flood season.

The oldest types of such dykes were made of beaten earth strengthened by stakes or beams: today they are made of cement blocks and metal baskets filled with stones.

But the river water, carrying with it detritus of all kinds, erodes, scrapes, demolishes and the dykes are in serious danger. It is therefore necessary to keep a careful and continuous watch on these protective works.

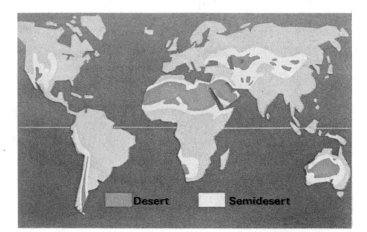

Desert   Semidesert

Why dams are built

Many watercourses do not have a constant flow: periods of flood alternate with periods of low water according to the season and this could bring industry and electric power stations to a complete standstill.

But man found a remedy for this: all he had to do was to close the valley through which the water ran by a dam so that the water could accumulate and form an artificial lake, a valuable reservoir for bad times.

The use of dams and embankments goes back to remote times. The Indians built them 5,000 years ago and in ancient Egypt some very imposing ones were constructed of stone. These lakes provided a convenient reserve of water for the dry season and irrigation could then continue even in summer.

With the discovery of electricity and the turbines for making it, dams multiplied rapidly. Today many stretches of valley in mountainous regions have been transformed by the patient and intelligent work of man into picturesque and useful lakes.

By means of pipes these lakes feed with absolute regularity power stations lower down the valley; many such dams are to be found, real masterpieces of engineering skill.

Sometimes, however, even the strongest dams give way to unusual forces of nature and then the water rushes down carrying destruction and death.

Among the most notable dams are the Aswan Dam across the river Nile, the Boulder Dam on the Colorado, and the Kariba Dam on the Zambesi.

Why lakes vary in size and shape

Lakes are found in nearly every kind of surroundings but are most abundant in high latitudes and in mountainous regions. They are also common along rivers and in the lowlands near to the sea. They vary considerably in size and may be either fresh or salt water; some are even more salty than the sea.

In the course of its long history the Earth has undergone numerous changes. The crust has risen frequently, splitting in many places and causing folds and depressions sometimes of immense size.

These movements of the Earth's crust are the origin of one kind of very deep and vast lake, which is very common, especially in Africa. Some of them, like the Caspian and the Dead Sea, are so big that they deserve the name of seas.

The Kariba dam on the Zambesi

107

Welsh lake

Why some lakes are of glacial origin

More than a million years ago, for reasons which we do not yet fully understand, the Earth became cold and glaciers covered a large part of the continents. In the valleys and basins the enormous masses of ice eroded the ground by their slow movement over it and dug out great hollows. They also pushed along in front of them large masses of stones and soil.

These masses of material, called moraine, formed real walls at the foot of the glaciers and as the glaciers retreated they became a barrier in the way of water coming down from the mountains. Lakes were formed in this way and were called glacial lakes because of their origin. They filled the hollows scooped out by the glaciers and were hemmed in by the old moraines.

There are other lakes, sometimes quite small, caused by the blocking of valleys or watercourses by various means.

Mounds of lava, glaciers, landslides, many natural obstacles can block a valley and prevent the water from flowing freely away. A lake is then formed above the barrier which may persist for a long time or may disappear as soon as the water succeeds in finding another way out down the valley.

Sometimes such lakes formed among the mountains are very beautiful and become famous tourist attractions.

The various shapes of lakes are therefore due to the nature of the terrain surrounding them and the particular character of the confining walls.

Often in the course of time lakes change their shape to some extent. This can happen, for instance, when part of their basin is filled with detritus carried down by the rivers which transform them into alluvial plains.

Why some lakes are called crater lakes

Crater lakes are those which occupy the craters of old extinct volcanoes or lie in hollows where several old volcanic outlets emerge.

Generally, because of their origin, crater lakes are circular in shape and are never very large. Nor are they usually very deep. They can have streams running into and out of them but there are some crater lakes which do not appear to be fed by any running water.

Some crater lakes, especially in America, have unusual features (hot water, sulphur water and so on) which are connected with previous volcanic activity.

Why there are many extinct volcanoes

In a volcano we can distinguish the following parts: the chimney formed of a number of irregular passages through which the white hot material comes to the surface; the crater or external mouth; the cone formed of ejected volcanic material. Often several secondary craters can open in the sides of the volcano, each with its own cone.

When a volcano ceases both its main eruptive activities (lava and stones) and also its secondary activity (smoke and sulphurous gases) it is said to be extinct but it is by no means unknown for a so-called extinct volcano suddenly to come to life again. The eruption of Vesuvius in A.D. 79 is an example of this, for the volcano had been dormant from the earliest recorded times.

The reason why a volcano ceases to be active is not yet quite clear: it is probably due to the chimney becoming blocked by a subsidence of the Earth's crust.

Volcanoes are distributed on the Earth's surface mostly in long series and these volcanic zones are at the edges of the huge sections or plates of rock that make up the Earth's crust.

The chief line of volcanoes is the Pacific Fire Belt which stretches almost all around the Pacific Ocean. The North-South Atlantic chain is composed of a line of volcanoes extending in the Atlantic Ocean from one Pole to the other. The Mediterranean chain comprises the volcanoes of the Carib-

bean, of the Mediterranean and of some Asiatic regions. Finally the African chain extends along the Great Rift Valley of the African lakes.

Why hot springs are found in some areas

There are two different phenomena where water and gases are ejected from cracks in the Earth: those in which the jet is continuous, called fumaroles, and those where the jet is intermittent, called geysers.

The first are vents from which continuous volcanic vapours issue at a high temperature carrying with them boric acid and other salts.

Industry makes use of fumaroles as a source of both thermal energy and boric acid.

Geysers, on the other hand, are hot springs which spurt jets of water and steam into the air. These jets sometimes exceed 100° of heat and rise as high as 50 metres at intervals ranging from a few minutes to several hours.

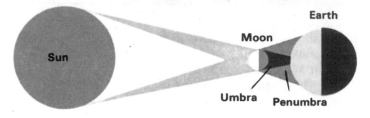

Eclipse of the Sun (below). In the area of the umbra there is a total eclipse and in the penumbra a partial eclipse.

Sun

Moon

Earth

Umbra   Penumbra

Total eclipse of the Sun

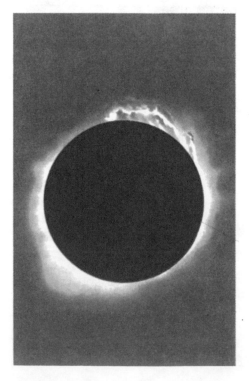

Why eclipses of the Sun and Moon occur

Eclipses of the Moon and of the Sun have been the subject of study from the earliest times. The Sun used to be regarded as a benevolent deity and men were terrified when it suddenly became dark. Even today primitive peoples panic when an eclipse takes place, and animals show signs of extreme agitation. A total eclipse does not last very long, however; seven and half minutes at most.

Nowadays we know the exact mechanism which causes the partial or total darkening of the Sun or Moon. An eclipse occurs when, through their movements of rotation and revolution, the Earth and the Moon are in perfect alignment with the Sun. The illustration shows the position of the three heavenly bodies which causes a total eclipse of the Sun: the Moon is exactly in front of the Earth and prevents the direct rays of the Sun from reaching parts of the Earth's surface. If we are in line with its cone of shadow we have a total eclipse of the Sun, and the Moon appears like a dark disk completely covering the Sun. On the other hand if we are in the area of the penumbra, the eclipse will be partial.

An eclipse of the Moon happens when the Sun, Earth and Moon are in line so that the Earth's shadow obscures the Moon. Unlike eclipses of the Sun, these eclipses can be seen from large parts of the Earth – from any place where the Moon is visible at the time. A lunar eclipse may be total or partial and a total eclipse lasts for a maximum duration of 102 minutes. However, the Moon may still be faintly visible during totality.

Why the study of eclipses is important

To us the Sun appears to be the largest and brightest of the stars visible to the naked eye, but it is really one of the smallest and faintest.

The illusion arises because it is the nearest star to us: the next nearest is nearly 300,000 times as far away.

Modern science has confirmed what the ancients had already observed, that the Sun is of fundamental importance for us. This is not only because it makes life on Earth possible, but also because the phenomena and disturbances which take place inside it affect all the planets of the solar system, and these effects are sometimes very far-reaching.

The mysterious spots which can be seen on its surface and which are thought to increase in size every eleven years and then regress again, for instance, cause serious disturbance of radio transmissions and also seem to have some effect on climate.

The violent explosions which take place in the chromosphere, the most superficial part of the Sun, and throw up gigantic columns of incandescent gases upon the corona of the Sun, also have a great influence on life on Earth.

Whilst many things which occur in the Sun can now be observed directly by means of suitable instruments, those which happen in the Sun's corona and particularly in its rarefied extremities, can only be properly observed during an eclipse of the Sun. The Moon then covers the disc of the Sun, leaving only the corona showing with its protuberances and incandescent plumes.

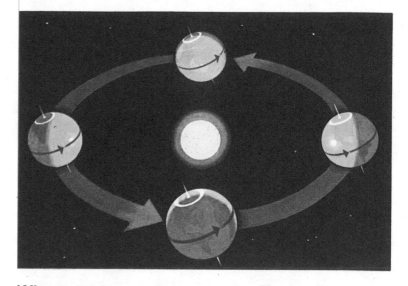

Why we have changes of seasons

The year is divided into four seasons which, in Europe, are associated with the annual pattern of plant life. They do not depend upon the greater or shorter distance of the Earth from the Sun, but on the varied inclination of the axis of the Earth at different times in relation to the Sun's rays.

Passing through the atmosphere the Sun's rays are filtered and cooled. The greater the distance to be travelled, the greater the amount of cooling.

For the same reason it is hotter on the equator than in other regions. Since the Earth is a sphere the Sun's rays are perpendicular at the equator and therefore pass through a shorter stretch of the atmosphere, whereas, when we approach the Poles, the rays become more oblique and cool down more.

The inclination of the axis of the Earth can correct this situation when the surface of one of the hemispheres moves into a more perpendicular position towards the Sun (it is then summer) or more inclined (and then it is winter).

The changing aspect of the Earth and its position relative to the Sun, produces the seasons.

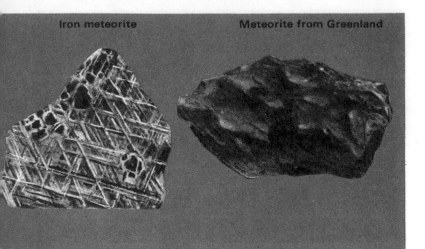

Iron meteorite   Meteorite from Greenland

or zones, each corresponding to the area between two meridians. In each zone the clock time changes.

As a starting point for numbering the meridians and the time zones the meridian chosen was the one which passes through Greenwich, where there is a very famous observatory.

Greenwich is therefore on zero longitude and from it follow the other meridians which divide the Earth into twenty-four segments each of 15°.

Why time is based on Greenwich

A day is the interval of time between two consecutive passages of the Sun over the same meridian, and it is therefore the result of the Earth's rotation.

As the passage of the Sun over the meridian of a place indicates mid-day it follows that whilst all the points on Earth on the same meridian have mid-day at the same time, other places will have mid-day at different times.

The difference is one hour for every 15° distance east or west (before and after). Because of this fact the Earth has been divided into twenty-four time segments

Why we see shooting stars at night

They are not really stars but meteors. We can see many of them at night, especially in August: they mark the dark sky with swift luminous traces and then disappear.

They are caused by meteoroids, masses of rock of various types, which approach the Earth from out of space. They can be of small size and slow speed or they may be a hundred metres in diameter and at very high speeds. What makes them luminous like stars is the Earth's atmosphere which causes friction enough to· burn them up completely before they reach the ground. That is why they disappear suddenly: they have been destroyed and no longer exist.

If, however, they are of exceptional size they may burst into flames in the atmosphere and be only partly consumed. If they do not explode in the final stage of their flight they will reach the surface of the Earth and will cause a crater similar to those on the Moon.

There are many theories regarding the origin of the thousands

The old observatory of Greenwich

of meteoroids which are to be found in space. The most probable would seem to be that of Schiaparelli, who considers that they are the results of the disintegration of comets. Swarms of them are found where a comet had been in orbit.

The meteoroids which fall on our planet are those which pass near to Earth and so come within the pull of the Earth's gravity.

Why there are craters on the surface of the Moon

We know that the craters which we can see on the Moon are for the most part due to meteoroids. All the bodies in space are subjected to a constant rain of meteoroids, large and small.

During the summer season the Earth passes through an area where meteors are very numerous. This phenomenon occurs around 10 August.

The meteoroids pass through the Earth's atmosphere, burst into flames because of friction against the molecules of the air, and most of them are completely destroyed before they reach the Earth.

Meteoroids which survive their fiery fall and strike the Earth's surface are called meteorites. Very few meteorites occur, and those that do hit the ground are usually very small. However, about 25,000 years ago, a meteorite made a huge crater in Arizona: 1,265 metres across and 175 metres deep.

In fact the Earth's atmosphere protects us from meteorites like a soft but very effective shield.

The Moon, on the other hand, has no atmosphere and therefore all the meteorites which it en-

counters land on its surface and cause craters. Sensitive instruments left behind by the astronauts now enable us to record with great accuracy the rain of meteorites which fall on the Moon.

Many of the small craters, in addition, are the results of volcanic effects, probably gases and dust which long ago escaped from the Moon's interior.

THE WHY OF ART

Why every nation has produced its own form of art

It was believed for a long time that the only valid and acceptable art forms were the classical ones, that is those produced by the western Greco-Latin civilizations. Any other forms of artistic expression were commonly regarded as the work of dabblers of little value. The sole exception was Egyptian art, which attracted universal attention chiefly because of the magnificence and size of its architectural works.

Today, however, many people consider that any form of art has its own intrinsic value and that there can be no question of any preconceived and universally accepted standards for judging the validity of all the varied artistic manifestations. In fact every nation has produced its own special type of art, different from all the others, because the spirit has been different which has animated artists, different also the culture in which they lived and by which they were influenced, and different, in particular, the inspiration which springs from a world always different and irrepeatable.

The truth of this can be seen when we consider that even artists belonging to the same nation, to the same culture and to the same tradition have produced different forms of art during their various periods of history.

Why artistic inspiration is often derived from religion

From rock drawings to the most modern forms of art we find throughout human history that religious faith has inspired innumerable artists in every field: from painting to architecture, from sculpture to mosaics.

The reasons for this are quite clear. Man has always had a strong belief in something transcendental, that is in something superior to himself, some power or powers to which he feels himself linked by profound spiritual bonds. To express through art his own interior world signified very often to approach divinity, to glimpse a part, even if only a very small part of it, in some way to share in it.

It was inspiration of a religious nature which moved the architects of all the temples in the world, the sculptors both known and unknown of the innumerable statues of divinity, the painters who adorned the places of worship, the tombs, the dwellings of the religious orders.

Even though today the world of scientific techniques has led men to considerations of a practical nature, artistic inspiration based on a religious faith, whichever it may be, has not lessened, although, as is to be expected, it has taken on new characteristics in tune with the times. Coventry Cathedral is an example of how religion has inspired modern artists.

Why we find the mother figure represented so much among the primitives

One thing above all else dominated the mind of primitive man: the survival of the race. The very hard life he was compelled to lead, the dangers surrounding him, the high rate of infant mortality, all developed in him the instinct of self-preservation, which was translated into a profound respect for fertility.

In the eyes of artists motherhood therefore assumed a magical and propitiatory significance. This can be seen from cave drawings and paintings but above all from the numerous small statuettes of pregnant women which have been found among so many different peoples.

The mother about to give life to another creature, the symbol of fertility, represented the hopes of the tribe and guaranteed its survival.

Why the Egyptians built tombs in the form of pyramids

In ancient Egypt the pharaohs were regarded as divine and were accorded the greatest veneration.

In this lies the reason behind the story of the pyramids. Some 3,400 years before Christ the tombs were covered with mounds of earth. In order to distinguish them from the tombs of ordinary mortals the tombs of the pharaohs were covered with a tumulus of bricks visibly larger than on others.

Four hundred years later, that is about the year 3000 B.C., the architect Imhotep was commissioned to build a special tomb for the pharaoh Zoser at Saqqarah. He placed a series of tumuli one on top of the other, each smaller than the previous one so as to form steps on the four sides. This was the first step pyramid of Egypt. The first pointed pyramid was built about 300 years later by the pharaoh Cheops at Giza.

Why the colours of rock paintings have lasted until now

The actual nature of the limestone forming the caves which our remote ancestors chose for their paintings has ensured that they

have been preserved and very often improved.

This is how the Stone Age artist produced his work: first of all he cut into the rock face the outline of the figure with flint chisels or knives and then he filled in these incisions and often the whole figure as well with colour. Drawing and painting, therefore, arose as twin arts, each complementing the other.

The commonest colours were red, black, brown and yellow; this was inevitable as these colours are provided by nature in the form of mineral oxides and fossil carbon.

In the course of time the primitive painters began to mix their colours with animal fats and other oily substances and then spread them over the figures like pastels. If the wall was very rough they blew on the colours directly by means of a bone tube. The limestone then slowly absorbed the colours and the moisture kept them fresh and bright.

Why some wall paintings are called frescoes

A fresco is a special technique for painting on walls. The name indicates the nature of this type of painting, for it means fresh, that is to say, painting straight on to a wall on which the plaster is still wet.

The painting of frescoes probably originated and was developed most in Italy, and takes advantage of a special characteristic of lime: this is mixed with water and sand to produce a cement which will absorb the colours spread on its surface while it is still fresh. The colours dry and set with the plaster and become a permanent part of the wall.

The artist who devotes himself to this type of painting must have a perfect knowledge of the technique which requires great speed of execution to prevent the fresco from drying, and a sure hand as it is not possible to make corrections or to do any retouching.

To give the work smoothness and polish special marble rollers are used to smooth down the walls.

Why we use the terms oil paintings, tempera and water colours

To amalgamate the pigments and enable the artist to use them for painting special substances known as binders are needed.

Oil is one of the commonest substances used for this purpose, and may be walnut, hemp or poppy oil. To make the pigments flow better linseed oil is also used together with turpentine and lavender oil. Oil paintings are characterized by mellow and brilliant colours.

The binders used for the pigments known as tempera are gums, glues and even wax dissolved in volatile oils. Sometimes, particularly during the fifteenth century, the pigments were mixed with egg yolk. Today we use animal glues kept fluid in a water bath.

Water colours use pigments diluted in gums. With these it is necessary to know exactly how much water to use to dilute the colours. The uniformity of the shades depends upon this ability. Years of experience are needed in order to succeed in this apparently commonplace activity. That is why many people think that painting in water colours is the most difficult.

Why clothes chests were sometimes painted or carved

The furnishings of private houses were very modest in olden times. In the Middle Ages wood workers began to make furniture of some artistic style and beauty but it was

not until the Renaissance that the art of making furniture really began.

Among the most typical articles to be found in a house during the Renaissance period was the clothes chest. This was a wooden chest fitted with a lid and short legs. It was used as a bench for sitting on and so was sometimes provided with a back and arms, and it was also a place for storing dresses and linen. It became the habit to give a clothes chest, decorated and painted in oils or carved, to the bride as part of her dowry. These chests were real works of art and quite valuable articles in themselves.

Why a model is prepared before making a sculpture

Before producing the final work the sculptor makes models, or trial efforts, and when these have been done to his satisfaction he then moulds the final work.

For the models he uses materials such as plasticine and clay and works these materials into the desired shape. In larger sculpture an inner structure, or armature, is built to support the clay which might otherwise collapse under its own weight.

A single model is not always enough for the artist to give form to his inspiration. Frequently artists make and remake their models before selecting the final one. The model embodies the sculptor's artistic conception and is the first essential step towards the work of art.

King Kata Mbula, 109th King of the Bakuba (Africa)

Why marble for sculptures must be selected very carefully

The sculptor must select with the greatest care the block of granite which he wishes to shape. It must be strong enough to stand up to the countless blows of the chisel. Blocks of marble quite often contain flaws inside them which might cause the artist to have completely to re-do his work.

118

Another thing which can happen and which may appear obvious, is sometimes the cause of bitter surprise: that is verifying the size of the blocks. They must be able exactly to contain the sculpture and correspond exactly to the greatest measurements required. Then the sculptor uses his chisels and drills to transform the marble into the work of art already perfected in the model.

Why some sculptures are called low relief and some high relief

There is a particular type of sculpture in which the statue is not moulded completely, that is to say all round, but only in part: this is the so-called sculpture in relief.

Another distinction is that between high relief and low relief. In the first instance the sculptured figures stand out by about two-thirds from the flat background and in the second case the figures only project slightly.

This type of sculpture is very old and goes right back to the days of primitive art. Relief sculptures have been found in caves inhabited by men of the Stone Age.

Why casting is used in sculpture

The artist who wants to translate the plaster model into a bronze statue must prepare the cast.

First of all he spreads a uniform layer of wax on to the model and this adheres perfectly to the plaster. The whole is then covered with a paste of fireclay, that is heat resisting clay. A number of holes are made in this covering. The statue is then heated which causes the fireclay to harden and melts the layer of wax. This oozes out through the holes and creates a vacuum into which the molten bronze is then poured. As it cools the bronze takes on the shape desired by the artist. The work of art is then completed by cleaning and chiselling.

The head of a bronze statue of the goddess Roma

these wooden units by a similar but stronger and more durable material, stone. That is how stone pillars came about.

At first they were no doubt very rough, probably not even round, and without any decoration at all. In the course of time they became more beautiful and elegant and were improved by additions such as bases and capitals.

When stone buildings became fully developed, pillars were used more and more, sometimes alone and sometimes in groups, or merely as decorative elements without any practical function.

Why the column is one of the basic elements of architecture

It is very difficult to establish exactly when man changed from being a simple builder and became an architect; that is to say when he changed from artisan to artist. What is certain is that one of the original architectural concepts, probably the first, was the column.

The idea of arranging two or more supports, the columns, to carry another unit, the architrave, seems to have originated in the dawn of Egyptian civilization, that is about 5,000 years ago.

First of all they were rough columns without much grace surmounted by beams which were just as rudimentary. In the course of time, however, the builders' taste developed more and more perfect forms. This is not strange when we remember the very delicate functions which they have in the complex structure of the whole edifice.

As supporting structures it was inevitable that columns should have a position of pre-eminence both as functional units and as

Why stone pillars replaced wooden ones

The material used for building the first human habitations was wood. In fact, even today the houses of many backward peoples are still built of wood and straw.

In Mesopotamia primitive columns were made of bundled reeds and mud; by 3000 B.C. they were covered with small glazed tiles which were both waterproof and decorative.

In Europe the first columns were crude wooden posts.

The trunks of trees were used for holding up the roofs and supporting the outside walls, and these became gradually bigger and stronger.

However the durability of tree trunks was very limited and they rotted and had to be replaced; also they could easily be burned down. Gradually man replaced decorative ones. This depended to a large extent on the types, proportions and qualities of the columns if the building, in addition to remaining erect, is to express harmony, power and grace. This is shown by the countless columns which adorn buildings of all ages, from the imposing buildings of ancient Egypt to the grandiose buildings of modern reinforced concrete in which large numbers of columns continue to fulfil their supporting and decorative purposes.

Why columns were often decorated in various ways

In his work every artist gives expression to his inner drive. His feelings and attitudes are inspired by the world in which we live, by the customs of the people, the historical circumstances which characterize a nation in any particular epoch. Therefore works of art are a reflection of the world into which the artist was born.

This is true of all art but perhaps particularly so of architecture. For instance Egyptian columns are rich in decorations which reflected the world of

The Egyptians built their colossal temples by transporting enormous masses of stone by human labour.

nature: lotus flowers, palm leaves and figures of men and animals. It is the expression of a world full of fantasy, vivacity and mystery, which was ancient Egypt.

The columns of the Doric style, austere and powerful, free from decoration and adornment, reflected the way of thinking, sober but still rich in harmony and artistic intuition, of ancient Greece.

The Ionic columns, light and

121

The baths of Diocletian in Rome (A.D. 305): concrete and bricks faced with marble and stucco

Why the Romans substituted the arch for the architrave

An indispensible complement of the columns was the architrave, that is the supported part which rested on the columns and upon which was then placed the roof of the building. As a general rule the architrave was composed of a single block of stone which could be decorated or not according to the various styles.

In the course of time architects learned, however, that a system based on columns and architrave did not enable a large enough area of space to be covered over and free from obstacles. Even expanding the space between one column and the next did not solve the problem. First of all it was impossible to find marble architraves long enough and strong enough, and in the second place it would not be an aesthetic advantage.

The Romans resolved the problem by using the arch. This was not an original invention: the Assyrians and the Egyptians knew how to build arches but had never made effective use of them.

The Romans probably learned of the arch from the Etruscans who were masters of architecture and the first exponents of arch construction in Europe. They may well have passed on their knowledge to the Greeks as well as to the Romans.

Roman builders more than any others had the idea, which has proved to be correct, that the arch was the architectural feature of the future. They perfected its structure to such a point that they used it in all their buildings: from temples to amphitheatres, from baths to aqueducts, and, of course, in the triumphal arch.

graceful and with volute capitals, express the sentiments of a gentle and elegant people.

The Corinthian style columns, the style preferred by the Romans with the capitals decorated with ornate clusters of leaves at the sides, is the original expression of elegance and wealth.

Why architecture is regarded as an art

Although the art of building houses developed a long time after painting and sculpture, it achieved a high degree of aesthetic value in a short time.

If an artist is one who translates his imagination into visible works, the architect can be regarded as an artist when he is able to enliven architectural forms with his inspiration. The more his work pleases and stimulates those who admire it, the more he can consider his aim as achieved and his inspiration realized.

In architecture as a form of art, one can never dissociate the technical element from the aesthetic. Anyone who wants to build a house, must have very precise scientific knowledge ranging from statics (the science of weight and of balance) to building materials, mathematics and geometry.

It will be true art, however, only if to such knowledge there is added a special flair for arranging the masses, for balancing the solids and the spaces, in adding elegance to shape, in arranging and balancing all the different aspects of decoration.

Why the keystone is the most important element in the arch

It is said that the arch used in building was taken from the shape of the bow used in archery. The curve of the arch is exactly that of the bow when it is bent under the pull of the string.

But what is the principle on which the arch, and the vault also, is based? The very elementary factor of the weight. The blocks or wedge stones of which the arch is made adhere together and support one another because they bear by their weight upon the two columns which support them: the bricks on the right upon the right hand column and those on the left upon the left hand column.

At the top, however, there is a brick or stone which has a special purpose. It thrusts to both right and left, thus forming the decisive point of equilibrium of the arch: without it neither arch nor vault could stay up and that is why it is called the keystone. In Etruscan, Roman and Renaissance arches it often projects slightly and is decorated with scrolls or figures.

Why we talk of semicircular and lancet arches

As soon as the arch had been discovered builders began to intro-

duce variations, some of them quite considerable. It remained a feature of architecture but was adapted to the style of various periods.

The first type to be developed and the commonest in Rome was the so-called semicircular arch, that is one which is a perfect half circle. Numerous examples of this can be seen in buildings of almost every period.

The other very usual type of arch is the pointed arch, also known as the lancet arch. It is made by two curved lines which join at the top to form an acute angle. This type was widely used during the Gothic period when a great variety of arch forms occurred.

In the rebuilt choir of Canterbury Cathedral (after 1174) architects used arcs of different size and radius to produce lopsided arches and even introduced angles into the arc.

Why Romanesque art flourished in the Middle Ages

Christian art, from the humble beginnings of the catacombs to the impressive art of the basilicas, had not given expression to anything new or really original.

It is true that a certain monotony in architecture had to some extent been corrected by the Byzantine influence but this was confined almost exclusively to interiors, rich with gold, enamel and multicoloured mosaics. Exteriors had remained very modest if not actually rough, with the sole exception of the cupola which, when well placed, could be beautiful and effective.

However in the time of Charlemagne a new style, particularly in architecture, began to spread very quickly, the Romanesque. Its name indicates one definite influence, that of Roman art. Solidity, clarity of line, elegance, a prevalence of solid planes over openings gave an impression of majestic and solemn calm of the classical type.

Why the flying buttress was widely used in Gothic architecture

The Romanesque architects, mostly monks, were very clearly influenced by the spirit of asceticism which yielded little to imagination, nature or inspiration. Their art was certainly sublime but it was also cold.

At the time when the Romanesque was reaching its peak in the twelfth century, a new style came from France, the Gothic. Its aspiration was obvious; a longing for height, vertical lines, delicacy and lightness.

But this explosion of inspiration and imagination had to come to terms with the inexorable laws of statics. Verticality, the prevalence of hollows over solids demanded completely new solutions. Supporting walls to carry the weight of the tall building would have had to be so thick that they would have spoiled the lightness of line which was the dominant feature of this style.

New solutions were therefore studied. First of all the semicircular arches and vaults were transformed into pointed ones to reduce the proportions of weight bearing on the support structures.

A system of supports was evolved to give stability and security to the vital points of the edifice. These supports took the form of thrusts provided by the so-called flying buttresses. They were arches or half-arches which rested upon strong and high buttresses, soaring upwards to the vital points needing support and reinforcement.

Why some buildings are called Flamboyant

The innumerable fluted columns, the abundance of windows, rosettes, tiny belfries and stone tracery, the presence of imposing but airy flying buttresses, the prevalence of pointed vaults and arches are the features which distinguish the Gothic style.

Such was the architects' zeal for buildings with lightness that more than once the buildings collapsed before they were finished. Nevertheless the new style had found its place and had been accepted. Until the coming of the

Construction of an old cathedral

Renaissance and beyond, the Gothic style produced some immortal works of art throughout Europe.

But, as so often happens, in the course of time the style became more complicated. In the attempt to become too beautiful it became affected and unstable. Gradually, unrestrained fantasy took over, resulting in works where the search for ornamentation, tracery, trimmings and virtuosity led to an over-abundance of decorative elements which often fell into affectation and artificality.

Hence the name of Flamboyant was given to this method of interpreting the original inspiration.

It may seem strange that just at the moment when it was taking on more refined forms, a style should become decadent when it had originally been called, clearly in a depreciative sense, Gothic, that is barbaric.

Why the style of the eighteenth century was called Neo-Classic

As with all human activities which are subject to recurrent tastes and reversions, in art the fever of the Baroque was succeeded by a period of reaction.

Palladian villa

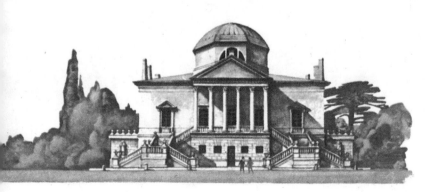

In architecture the tumult of Baroque lines gave way to sobriety and classical simplicity. It was a return to origins, to the inspirations of that classical refinement which Western culture regards as its source. That is why the term Neo-Classic is used, meaning the new classical style which began from about the year 1700 onwards.

The Renaissance was also a period of classical rediscovery, of a return to certain aesthetic criteria, but of much larger scope because enriched by another and different inspiration.

The Neo-Classical style, freed from the robust sense of art which characterized the Renaissance, was reduced to a cold and formal return to the classical. Its buildings were solid, linear and rather severe, tending towards archaeological precision. Often they were merely uninspired copies of ancient monuments.

The movement was towards simplicity and rigidity, and some people wished to abandon all decoration, even classical decoration.

Why the Renaissance is regarded as the richest period of art

Towards the middle of the fifteenth century geographical discoveries, new inventions, the intensification of scientific study instead of philosophy signalled the end of the Middle Ages.

A new age was born in which men rediscovered the values of reason, reality and nature. Free from the preconceptions and fears of the Middle Ages and favoured by a period of relative peace, culture turned again to the beauty of the Greek and Roman classical periods.

People became aware that life was beautiful and should be lived intensely, so that the pleasures of the spirit and the refinement of aesthetic taste dominate this period, the Renaissance.

Architecture, like all the arts, translated this spirit of rebirth into unequalled beauty. A harmonious combination of mediaeval and classical forms, the architecture of the Renaissance acquired a spirit of elegance, solemnity and strength. Its fundamental law was the rational investigation of reality which was the most important contribution of the period. In this reality there was no place for excessive ornamentation; it was dominated by the laws of perspective which created order and proportion, harmonious elegance, grandeur and purity of line.

The Renaissance initiated the modern age by expressing as an aesthetic whole all that was most perfect in human achievement at that time.

Why there are so many Baroque churches in Latin America

The Spanish conquerors and colonizers of America were almost always accompanied by Roman Catholic priests who, in addition to acting as chaplains to the Spaniards, set up new native Christian communities.

In the course of this colonization, South America became enriched with religious buildings. It was natural that the dominant style of these buildings should be the one most in favour in seventeenth-century Spain.

So it came about, as a result of the work of the colonizing priests, many of whom were Jesuits, that the Baroque style which dominated the European artistic scene in the seventeenth century, spread throughout America.

How did this style arise? The rare perfection of Renaissance art, its stupendous balance of forms, had ended by falling into affectation. A new idea in art was born which according to its founder, the Italian poet Giambattista Marino, should arouse wonder and surprise. From such ideas arose an art completely devoted to creating grandiose works, unexpected, even spectacular.

Architecture was also strongly influenced by it: no more classical simplicity but exuberant decoration, no longer clarity and purity of line but grotesqueness and virtuosity. In short it was the triumph of irregularity and caprice. All this is indeed shown in the name of this style, Baroque, which in Spanish means irregular.

Peruvian church
of the sixteenth century

127

Why modern architecture is different from the old

The technical problem which has worried builders of all periods more than any other is that of statics. Obviously the prime function of a building is to stay erect: if it tumbles down it ceases to be a building.

The problems of statics have always been closely connected with aesthetic problems. In other words, the stability of a building must not be imperilled by its design. Often for this reason some very original, even audacious, solutions were proposed, but always within very limited margins.

The age of daring buildings, of dizzy heights and shapes which seem to defy all the laws of equilibrium and statics, could not begin until the discovery of reinforced concrete.

This revolutionary invention in the building industry is based on some very elementary principles. Building materials must possess two important qualities: resistance to compression and resistance to traction. The mixture of cement, sand and gravel which is called concrete is very resistant to compression but not very resistant to traction. On the other hand, iron is very resistant to traction and not so much to compression. The combination of these two materials, concrete and iron, gives the best results as regards both compression and traction.

Buildings have therefore arisen in which the supporting structure is made of concrete reinforced by iron rods of various sizes.

Modern architects can in this way develop bold and very original buildings. Some well known examples of what can be achieved with reinforced concrete are to be found in the futuristic buildings in the new city of Brasilia.

Among the men who have produced real works of art in reinforced concrete are Frank Lloyd Wright, Alvar Aalto and Le Corbusier. To these three we owe much of the inspiration of modern architecture.

Modern opera house, Sydney

Skyscraper, New York

128

Why there is a great variety of architectural styles

It might logically have been thought that with the establishment of modern architecture all the buildings would be of the same style. This sometimes seems to be the case in the new parts of our cities.

But what determines the development of different styles, even when the building techniques remain the same, is the diversity of inspiration. Every type of culture produces its own forms of art, just because the culture of a people is the combination of situations, sentiments, traditions, resonances, and, therefore, also of inspiration, all of which are original and unique.

It cannot be denied, however, that there is today a tendency for culture to become uniform, particularly because of the enormous growth in communication through the press, radio, television and so on. Nevertheless, there will always be a place for original works of art.

Modern building in Canada

It is time to go back to a natural order and scale if man is to find himself, his human personality, his capacity and joy of living.

The more sensitive architects have understood these needs and have to some extent faced up to the problems which they present. As a result garden cities have arisen, which make the cities more spacious and airy and avoid their becoming human ant heaps.

Why the cities of the future may be like gardens

An idea which is rapidly gaining ground in the field of architecture is that which provides for the better placing of human dwelling places in a framework of natural surroundings, making them quiet, comfortable and relaxing.

Nowadays, in fact, buildings run the risk of dehumanizing people by shutting them up in enormous over-populated blocks, veritable human hives, with no contact with plants and trees, the real background which nature provides for man.

The Palace of Congresses, Brasilia

Why Chinese porcelain is famous

When Marco Polo returned from China and brought back to the West the first articles of porcelain, the alchemists throughout Europe vied with one another to discover the secret of its composition.

As a result it became known that Chinese porcelain is composed of two main ingredients; kaolin and petuntse.

The first is a very well known white clay and the second is a rock which becomes vitreous, or transparent like glass, only if raised to a temperature of about 1,500°C.

It is this substance which makes possible the production of hard paste porcelain. In addition during firing a special varnish combines perfectly with the paste on to which it is spread and gives it a very special finish.

The Chinese refer to the clay as 'the bones' of the vessel and the petuntse, or vitrifying substance, as 'the flesh'.

The success of Chinese porcelain was so great that when it first appeared in Europe it became just as valuable as precious metals like gold and silver.

Why enamels are used with certain metals

The precious metals which are used for making jewellery have been embellished since very ancient times by setting stones in them and by enamels. Fine gold and pure copper as thin as possible are the best metals on which to enamel.

Enamels are multi-coloured vitreous glazes which enhance the appearance of objects and make them particularly valuable.

The enamel is coloured by means of metallic oxides and is fused directly on to the surface to be decorated.

Why precious stones are cut

Some stones are called precious because they have qualities of special hardness, beauty and rarity.

In olden days magical properties were attributed to precious stones and it was believed that in some way they were connected with divinity. In the natural state these stones are found in the form of rough minerals. To give them their beauty, brilliance and transparency they have to be cut in a particular way. Diamond cutting, for example, was designed to take full advantage of all the light entering the gem and reflected from all the facets. The unit of weight of precious stones is the carat which is equal to one-fifth of a gramme or 3·163 grains.

Why man creates beauty in objects of every day use

As soon as ancient man had freed himself from the worries of survival, he turned his attention to work which was of no immediate practical use but served to make life more comfortable and beautiful. This is how, from the earliest times, pottery, bracelets, ornaments and jewellery began. In the course of centuries the art of the goldsmith, of porcelain, of miniatures, of engraving had attracted skilful craftsmen and artists. They knew how to create articles of daily use which still survive to this day in hundreds of museums and collections.

Why flower arrangement is also an art

Ikebana is a typically Japanese art. It consists in arranging flowers not merely for the aesthetic pleasure of their appearance but also to draw from them religious and philosophical inspiration and encouragement. *Ikebana* is therefore a true art form since it implies creation initiated by deep emotion.

Japanese flower arrangements are always subject to well defined rules based on predetermined ideas or themes.

In *ikebana* there are three main themes but they are very significant ones: heaven, man and Earth. Heaven is represented by a spray which dominates the composition in the vertical direction; man, who occupies the centre, is symbolized by flowers or leaves; the Earth then occupies the lowest space and is represented by vegetation combined with soil or moss.

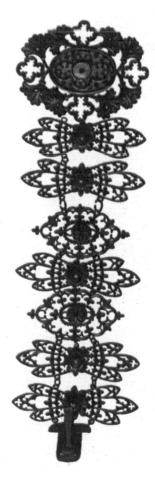

THE WHY OF MATHEMATICS

Why we cannot do without mathematics

How many times in a day's work do we have to use mathematics and calculations? It is difficult to say exactly but it is certain that there is no activity, however remote it may seem, that is not in some way connected with numbers.

Let us take a few examples from everyday life. Mother usually begins her day by thinking of what she will have to buy for the family's meals; father goes off to work and whatever means of transport he uses he will sooner or later need money; the children think of the times of their lessons, the time for play and the time to leave school; grandfather looks through the newspaper and cannot avoid getting involved in economic and financial articles. In short, the day has hardly begun and we have all come face to face with figures. By the end of the day the number of calculations done by each one of us will be quite considerable, even though we may not be aware of it. It may be a matter of mental arithmetic or done on paper, it may be easy or it may be difficult but it is all necessary for human existance. If this happens in our normal everyday life, what will happen in large professional or business concerns?

A numerical exercise is bound to be needed sooner or later: everything is indissolubly bound up with mathematics and calculations.

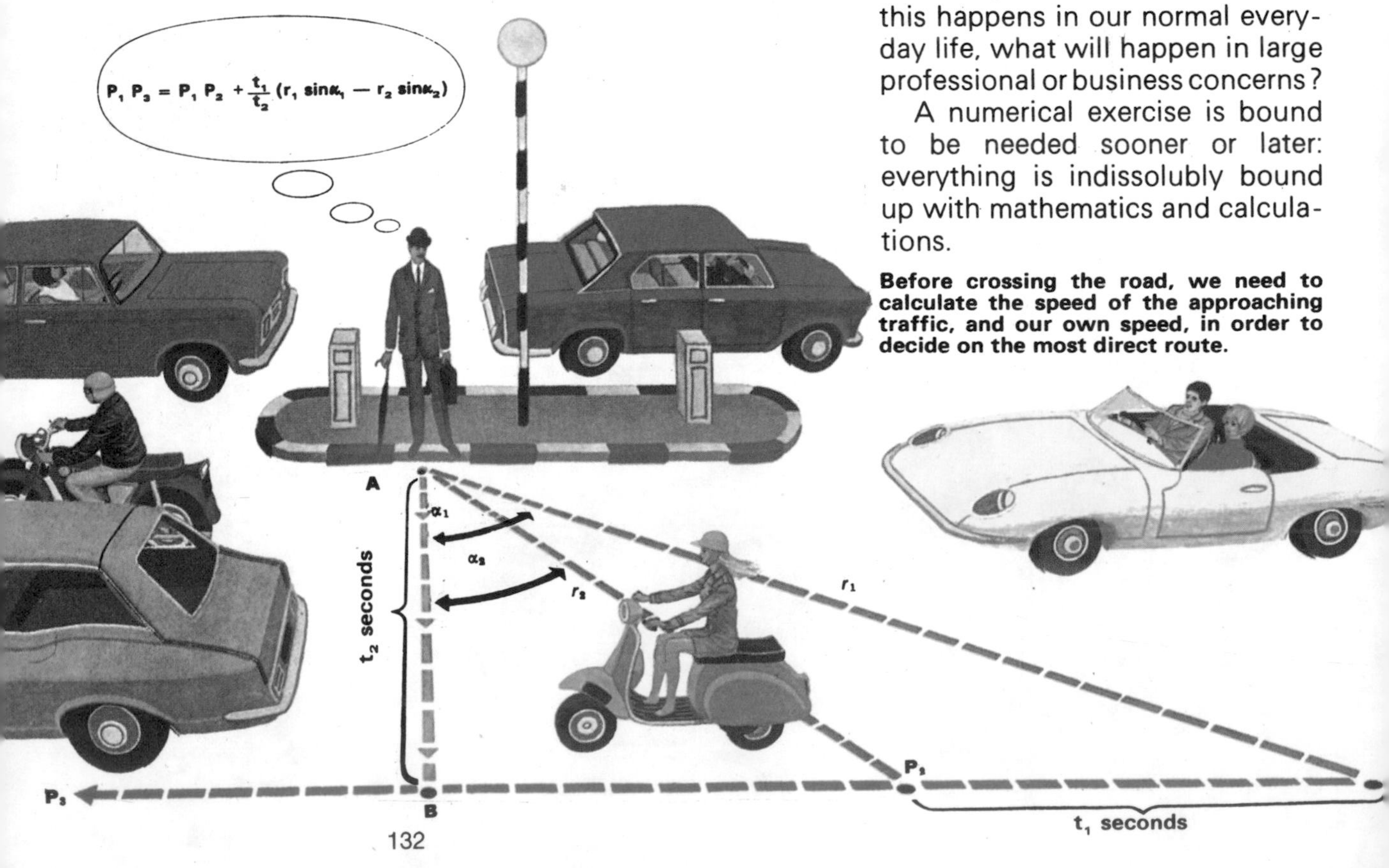

Before crossing the road, we need to calculate the speed of the approaching traffic, and our own speed, in order to decide on the most direct route.

$$P_1 P_3 = P_1 P_2 + \frac{t_1}{t_2}(r_1 \sin \alpha_1 - r_2 \sin \alpha_2)$$

A

α_1

α_2

r_2

r_1

t_2 seconds

B

P_3

P_3

t_1 seconds

Why we use the decimal system

If we wish to discover the origin of some of our old customs which date back to the very early days of our history, it is often very useful to look at habits and customs which still exist.

This is the case with numbers. Ethnologists, men who study man's history and origins, discovered that among primitive people counting is usually done on the fingers and sometimes on the toes as well.

This is probably the origin of the system of numbers and the method of calculation commonly in use among the majority of people today. Decimals began with the number of fingers on our hands. It was therefore a natural and spontaneous development: discovery and invention at the same time.

However, surprising as it may seem, according to the opinions of some experts and despite its natural origins, the decimal system is not as practical and convenient in use as systems of calculation based on the numbers six, twelve or twenty-four.

The decimal system, therefore, may be a natural thing but is not as simple as it might appear to those who have been accustomed to it from infancy.

Did all primitive peoples use the decimal system? Certainly not and there are people today who still use very different methods. The binary system, for instance, which is the basis for modern electronic calculators, was used by the Chinese more than 3,000 years ago and a rather complicated development of it is still in use among the Bengalis, who are regarded as expert calculators.

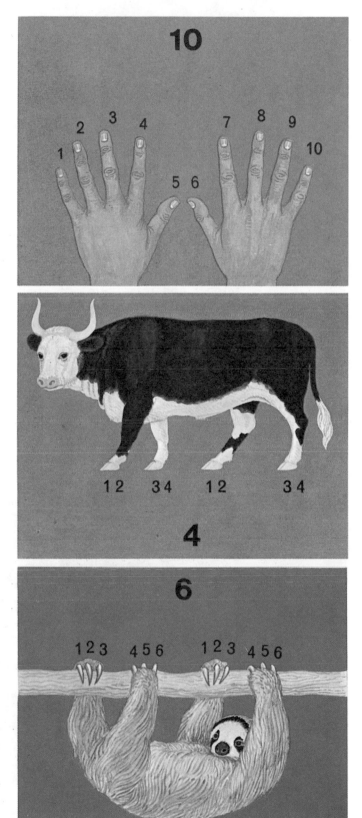

Why many primitive people only count up to twenty

Although a system of numbers based on our fingers and toes is in a certain sense the most convenient because the means of counting are always to hand, it can nevertheless be very limiting: in other words, there is a risk of never exceeding the number twenty.

This has happened among some backward peoples. The Australian aborigines, for example, usually count on the fingers and toes in this way; 1=one finger, 2=two fingers, 3=three fingers, 4=two fingers and two fingers, 5=half the fingers or one hand, 6=one hand and one finger, 10 = two hands, 15=two hands and one foot, 20=two hands and two feet. They inevitably stop at this point. To continue to count means to them to begin again from one and arrive once more at twenty.

Why the Babylonians were such good mathematicians

The civilization which developed in the area of the river Tigris and the river Euphrates reached its greatest splendour with the second Babylonian Empire about 2,500 years ago. At that time the Babylonians were distinguished from the other highly civilized nations around them by the intensive trading which they carried on.

Their foreign trade was perhaps the greatest factor which upheld the economy of the state. As they had no raw materials and widely used articles such as metals, timber, silk and spices, the Babylonians were forced to look for these things wherever they could be found. Trade on such a vast scale demanded a considerable knowledge of mathematics, and Babylonian merchants possessed this to a degree.

Why the Egyptians must have been good at geometry

Whenever we talk about ancient Egypt our thoughts immediately go to the huge buildings, the colossal monuments erected by the genius of this exceptional people. Pyramids, temples, sphinxes and obelisques could not be built by anyone who did not have an extensive knowledge of the laws of geometry.

The Egyptians were indeed surprisingly skilful in this science despite the fact that they had to rely for the necessary measurements on a system of calculation which was anything but rapid.

In the opinion of the Greek historian Herodotus (about 484 to 424 B.C.) who was well acquainted with Egyptian civilization, the origin of the study of geometry among this people is to be found in a colossal undertaking which was often repeated, that is the measuring of the land, and that is how this science got its name: geometry means measurement of the Earth.

Every Nile flood brought with it the benefit of very fertile mud but at the same time it also washed away all the boundary marks between the various properties and divisions of land. After every flood, therefore, it was necessary to repeat all the observations, measurements and divisions to restore things to their previous state.

From this very practical need to measure and remeasure the ground arose, it seems, the Egyptian interest in geometry. Measurement of the ground was connected with another very important factor, the payment of taxes which were based on the amount of land which a man possessed.

Ancient Egyptian instruments for measuring time. The ancient Egyptians were among the first people to recognize the need for measuring instruments of all kinds. The particular natural conditions in Egypt, where the Nile caused continual flooding, meant that they had constantly to recalculate the divisions of land and property.

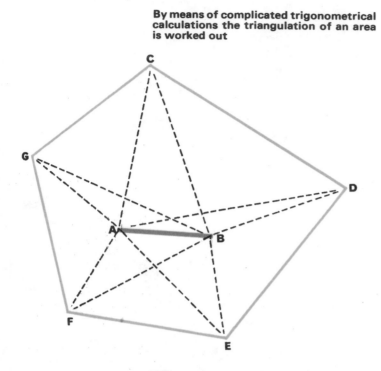

Why we use triangulation for measuring fields

The measurement of areas of land would be quite easy if they were always symmetrical.

It becomes complicated when irregular shapes have to be measured. That is where triangulation comes to our aid. It is a method of land surveying by which the position of one or more points is located by the use of trigonometrical calculation. The procedure consists in fixing an initial base line, which is normally the distance between the point of observation and a predetermined point. This is the base line of a triangle, possibly equilateral, the sides of which in turn form the base lines for adjacent triangles. Further calculations and the use of special surveying instruments enable an exact measurement to be made of these triangles.

If it is necessary to determine the points of a very large area, the space is first divided up into a number of triangles lying side by side and originating on the base line. By taking the exact measurement of one side and calculating the angles, all the distances of the specified points can be determined by means of trigonometrical calculations.

Triangulation, a very ancient art, still remains fundamentally unchanged.

All the calculations needed for measuring fields are based directly on the theorem of Pythagoras and can be demonstrated by it

Why geometric symbols abound in magic

From very ancient times mathematical calculations and geometrical studies were the almost exclusive prerogative of certain classes of people, who were surrounded by the aura of mystery and magic which always accompanies those who are able to do unusual things.

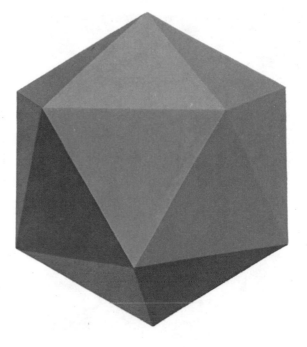

Among the Egyptians, for example, the experts in these matters were the priests. Because of their studies they were able to direct the building of the great temples and colossal tombs thereby giving considerable impetus to the advancement of learning. But their art was strange and secret, full of numbers, formulae and symbols which were mysterious because they were incomprehensible to most people.

Many of the monuments which they devised were, in fact, excellent astronomical laboratories by which they obtained information regarding the movements of the stars. Through such knowledge they created in the people a superstitious respect for divinity and reflected honour for themselves.

The magico-religious world was thus always dominated by symbols and figures of mathematical origin. It was a world of symbols which were well known to the experts but which were believed by the ordinary people to be sure signs of magic, incomprehensible and therefore capable of all kinds of influences, mostly negative.

Countless mysteries existed in this world of superstition and were characterized by an infinite number of signs and symbols. Spheres, circles, triangles, prisms, cabalistic numbers have always been the essential stock-in-trade of any magician worthy of the name, the tools of his trade.

By means of these instruments he, so to speak, made concrete the thousands of questions, fears and mysteries which beset the mind of the superstitious individual.

The crystal ball has always been important in magic

Leonardo da Vinci; a great scientist and artist

Most of our figures were first used in India. The Arabs learnt of them at the end of the eighth century and in about 825 a small book appeared on the subject. This was translated into Latin by Abelard of Bath around 1120, and Arabic figures were introduced into European arithmetic during the Middle Ages.

The new method of counting, based on simple rules, produced not only cultural but also practical benefits because it facilitated trade and commerce.

Why nought is the most important numeral

The figure nought which we use with such ease and assurance was unknown among the ancients and was introduced only with the system of calculation devised by the Indians. It did not become known in the West until about the twelfth century.

The symbol nought was soon recognized as more important than the other figures. With it, it is possible to indicate various mathematical situations, some of them very complex, for example in connection with decimals. First of all nought is used to indicate that in a whole there are no units. If, for example, there are not any balls in a box, we say that there are no balls. Nought is also the result of subtracting two equal numbers. By taking away three balls from a heap consisting of three balls, the result is no balls. Secondly the use of nought makes it possible to express any number, however large and complex, by means of the other nine numerals. The difference between our system of numbers and other systems which do not have a nought, as

Why we use Arabic numerals

The Arabs, Persians, Egyptians and Hindus have all claimed to be the originators of what we call Arabic numerals. But perhaps it was the traders who carried these symbols from one country to another so that our numbers came together from several different sources.

for instance that of the Romans, is clear.

The nought, like the other nine numerals, has more than one meaning. For example in the number 250 its value is quite different from that in the number 205 although exactly the same figures are used in both. In the Indo-Arabic system the value of a figure depends upon its position but only the nought has no numerical value but still has a positional value. The numeral nought has quite rightly been defined as a small number of enormous importance.

Why the human mind cannot understand the exact meaning of some numbers

If, after counting up to twenty, the Australian aborigine wishes to express a large number he merely says 'many'.

Confronted with the number 1,000 million many of us would begin to feel like the aborigine. Purely as a matter of curiosity if we wished to count 1,000 million pounds, pound by pound, it would take us seventy years.

What can be said, then, about a light year? That is, the distance travelled by light in 365 days. In round figures, light travels at a speed of 300,000 kilometres a second; in a year it travels nearly 10 million million kilometres; can anyone comprehend such a distance?

The human mind is very limited when it comes to understanding very high numbers. It is true that we continue to calculate them even when they indicate colossal amounts, but we do so in purely mathematical terms, without being able to understand their full implication.

Why we say that mathematicians are very absent-minded

The traditional belief that studious people in general and mathematicians in particular are very absent-minded is supported by numerous stories.

Perhaps it is because, in the olden days, the science of calculating was closely connected with astronomy, and when one is interested in the stars it is logical to walk along the street with one's face turned towards the sky. The image of a studious person lost in the clouds was given by Plato

The symbol for nought was introduced by the Indians, adopted by the Arabs, and transmitted to Europe

himself. He said that many an astronomer finished by falling into a well because of his habit of looking upwards.

A very famous episode is that about Newton who, wanting to boil an egg when his mind was taken up with calculations, put his watch into the boiling water and timed it with the egg in his hand.

Why among ancient peoples there was a great similarity in the way numbers were written

Man's ability to make calculations is certainly very old. For instance, barter, the primitive form of trad-ing, required some form of calcula-tion, however elementary.

According to some scientists, however, it seems that primitive man made longer calculations to signify the passage of the days and months. He cut notches in a tree trunk or stick, short ones for

1	I	𒁹	A	•
2	II	𒁹𒁹	B	••
3	III	𒁹𒁹𒁹	Γ	•••
4	IIII	𒁹𒁹𒁹𒁹	Δ	••••
5	III II	𒁹𒁹𒁹 𒁹𒁹	E	▬
6	III III	𒁹𒁹𒁹 𒁹𒁹𒁹	F	▬•
7	IIII III	𒁹𒁹𒁹𒁹 𒁹𒁹𒁹	Z	▬••
8	IIII IIII	𒁹𒁹𒁹𒁹 𒁹𒁹𒁹𒁹	H	▬•••
9	III II III	𒁹𒁹𒁹𒁹𒁹 𒁹𒁹𒁹𒁹	Θ	▬••••
10	∩	◄	I	▬▬
100	ℓ	𒁹◄◄	P	⬭

Egyptian, Babylonian, Greek and Mayan numerical systems

the days and long ones for the months. One notch indicated a day, two notches two days, and so on.

It appears that from these notches originated the strokes which were used for counting. One significant proof of this is that the symbols in use among different nations bear a great resemblance to one another.

The Egyptians, who had papyrus leaves to write on, used a genuine stroke, as also did the Romans, but the Babylonians, who had to write on clay tablets, made wedge-shaped marks. The Mayas, on the other hand, were more expeditious and used dots.

Why the Romans could not do complicated calculations

Roman numerals, which are still in use for certain purposes, were rather rudimentary and perhaps that is why the Romans, who were very advanced in certain respects, were certainly no good at mathematics.

There were two great difficulties which they had to overcome in calculating: the somewhat complicated method of writing the signs and the lack of the figure nought. It is quite incomprehensible to us how they could ever carry out a simple multiplication such as 58 times 234. A task like this, which does not present any great difficulty to a school child, must have been rather complicated for them. For instance, the number 58 was written thus: LVIII, and the number 234: CCXXXIV.

Finally the lack of a nought among their figures complicated matters enormously.

It is a significant fact that although experts in the subject are able to explain quite clearly the Roman system of numerals they are quite unable to explain how calculations were done, particularly complicated ones with high numbers.

Why we can say that animals are able to count

It may seem rather strange to say that animals are able to count, but some interesting experiments have been carried out in this connection.

For instance a hen was fixed in such a way as to be able to peck and grains of corn were arranged in lines on a sheet of cardboard. The odd grains (1, 3, 5, etc.) were free but the even ones (2, 4, 6, etc.) were fixed firmly to the cardboard. In a very short time the hen learned to ignore the even grains and to peck contentedly only at the odd ones, one after the other. The experiment was varied by placing a free grain in every third position and the hen soon learned this lesson also. The same occurred with three and then four grains between the free ones. It was only after this that the bird became uncertain.

The number five may possibly be the limit to which the birds can count.

Crows never return to their nests if there is anyone near them. A hut was built near a crow's nest and a man went into it. The crow did not return until the man had left. Two men went in and the bird would not return until both of them left. This went on up to five, after which the bird became confused.

Why the decimal system is not used in computers

Since the introduction of Arabic numerals into Europe over seven hundred years ago, there has never been such a revolution in the world of mathematical calculations as that being brought about at the present time by computers.

Flow chart for automatic composition

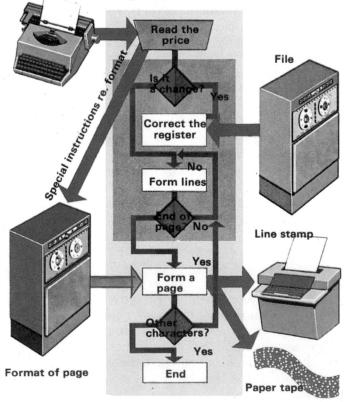

Read the price

Is it a change?   Yes

Correct the register

No

Form lines

End of page?   No

Yes

Form a page

Other characters?

Yes

End

Special instructions re. format

File

Line stamp

Format of page

Paper tape

Compared with these modern machines for quick and accurate calculations, the old counting rods invented by Napier in 1617 and the calculating machine invented by Pascal in 1642 and even the electric calculators in use for many years, are all like toys.

The first electronic computers were developed in Britain and America just over forty years ago, but they have already invaded every field of human science and are rapidly becoming indispensable instruments of progress.

Like all inventions, even computers have borrowed something from the past and added many new things to it. Among the things which have been discarded, one notable victim is the decimal system. It may seem strange not to use this old and well-tried system but the needs of a machine are different from those of a man.

The decimal system is very convenient for us but the complicated mechanisms of the computer prefer the binary system. The structure and operation of the circuits which are normally used in computers are much better adapted to the system based on two, and not ten like the decimal system.

In the binary system numbers are represented by the successive powers of two and every time a number is represented it has to be broken down to indicate the presence or absence of a certain power of two with a 'yes' or a 'no', with a one or a nought, with a dot or a line, and so on.

Above all else this system gives a better guarantee of perfection. In a binary circuit the probability of an error occurring is one in a million during the first thousand hours' operation.

Why computers need memories

The memory of a computer is the part of the computer in which it holds programs and also data. A program is a set of instructions that tell the computer to carry out a particular task. The data is the information that the computer needs to do this.

The computer has its own internal memory unit. The program is fed into the memory, normally by connecting a disk or tape drive to the computer. A magnetic disk or tape that contains the program is inserted into the drive. The data that the computer requires may also be on disk or tape, or the computer may ask the operator to enter the data required by using an input unit such as a keyboard. In all cases, the data also enters the computer memory. The computer's processing unit then follows the program and takes data from the memory to produce the results.

The computer's internal memory may lose all its programs and data when the computer is switched off. This is why they have to be stored on disks or tapes.

Why computers are often used in banks

The need for rapid communication between a central office and outlying branches is now under consideration in many spheres.

Among them are the banks. The branch offices are provided with electronic terminal apparatus for collecting information. By this means the banking operations transacted during the day are transmitted continuously to the head office which works out the total balance at the end of each day's activity. By this means rapid operations are possible which would otherwise require a great deal of time and would also be liable to more errors.

This control process is carried out with considerable economy since banks of different companies have the same banking systems.

Data system for banks

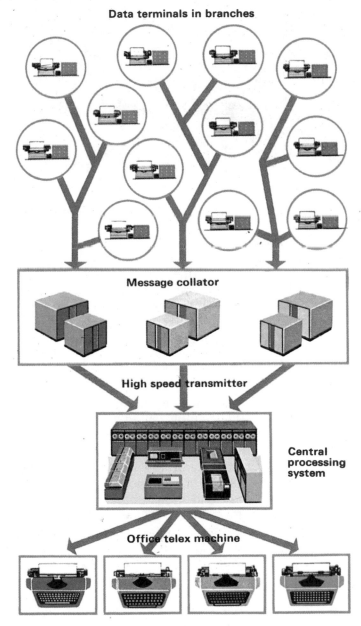

Data terminals in branches

Message collator

High speed transmitter

Central processing system

Office telex machine

The Feast of Herod by Israel van Meckenem

Why there are seven musical notes

Music based on the seven notes of the diatonic scale is only about a thousand years old. It was in fact invented by Guido d'Arezzo, a Benedictine monk who was extremely fond of sacred music and who lived from about 990 to 1050.

Until that time there were no real musical notes as such but only signs called neumes which means accents. They were used in singing to indicate the syllables on which the voice had to be raised or lowered.

The suggestion which led to the invention of notes was taken by Brother Guido from a Latin hymn dedicated to St. John. This hymn was composed of verses all of which began with a sound higher than the preceeding one. Guido used the syllables with which these verses commenced to construct the succession of sounds which we now know as the musical scale.

Here are the verses: *UTque laxis, REsonare fibris, MIra gestorum, FAmuli tuorum, SOLve polluti, LAbii reatum.* Later the UT was changed to DO and the seventh note TE was added.

A harpist from an Egyptian wall painting

Why there is a difference between solar time and sidereal time

We all know that the Earth moves in two distinct ways: one of revolution around the Sun and the other of rotation on its own axis. The first movement takes nearly 365 days and 6 hours and the second takes 24 hours.

There is a difference, however, between the solar day and the sidereal day. The solar day is calculated by measuring the time it takes the Earth to make one complete rotation around its axis, using the Sun as the point of reference. This time is exactly 24 hours. As each hour consists of 60 minutes and each minute of 60 seconds we can also say that a day is a period of 1,440 minutes or 86,400 seconds.

However, if instead of using the Sun as our point of reference we used a remote star, we would see that the Earth takes exactly 86,164 seconds for one complete rotation (sidereal time).

How can we explain this difference of 236 seconds? By the fact that while the Earth is completing one full rotation, it has moved a short distance on its journey around the Sun, to be precise 236 seconds.

Why our calendar is called Gregorian

The Gregorian calendar which still exists today is named after Pope Gregory XIII under whose pontificate the reform of the calendar was carried out. The earlier Julian calendar of Julius Caesar reckoned the year at 365 days and 6 hours which created a day extra every four years (leap

year). However, more precise calculations carried out by a special commission appointed by Pope Gregory established that the solar year was 365 days, 5 hours, 49 minutes and 46 seconds.

The time which had been lost in the course of years was recuperated on the night of 14 October 1582 when a leap forward of ten days was made.

Why liquids are measured in litres

The metre was made the only unit of measurement in France for measuring length with effect from 1 January 1840. It was the first but by no means the only stage in the decimal metric system, which also included measurements of volume and weight together with their accompanying multiples and submultiples.

Although the ancient peoples had made some progress in the measurement of length, for the measurement of capacity they were confined to using the hollow of the hand or some other extremely elementary container which did not form a constant unit.

The litre, the unit for measuring capacity in the metric system, is very closely linked to the metre. It is, in fact, the capacity of a container in the shape of a cube with sides measuring one decimetre, that is one-tenth of a metre. The litre is equal to about one and three-quarter pints.

The litre was too small and inconvenient to measure the contents of a large tank and multiples are therefore used: the decalitre or 10 litres and the hectolitre or 100 litres.

For measurements smaller than a litre we use the decilitre or one-tenth of a litre and the centilitre or one-hundredth of a litre.

Why distances are measured in metres

Throughout the centuries there have been many and varied systems of measurement. Gradually, however, man realized that if he wished to measure the things which interested him with any degree of accuracy he would have to use a constant unit of measurement.

Many different units of measurement were invented, but it was not until the end of the eighteenth century that the need to unify existing measures into a single practical system was studied with particular attention. In 1790 the French National Assembly put forward a plan for unifying all weights and measures.

The Paris Academy of Sciences was given the task of working out a new system. The special commission appointed by the Academy included the greatest scientists of the age and they decided unanimously to adopt as the unit of length a fraction of the Earth's meridian.

After seven years of meticulous research the unit was finally found: it was equal to one-forty millionth part of the Earth's meridian and was called a metre, which is a Greek word meaning measurement.

It took many years for the metric system to be accepted throughout France. Its progress in other countries has been slow and in 1875 an International Bureau of Weights and Measures was set up on international territory at Sèvres, near Paris.

Except for North America, the metric system is now in use throughout the world.

Why weights are measured in grammes

It is probable that the need for a unit of weight was only clearly realized when trading in precious metals began. It was one thing to calculate the approximate weight of a sack of corn or a calf but quite a different matter to work out the weight of a quantity of gold, silver or precious stones.

There are many things which seem to point to the fact that the first measurements of weight were very small. Even today we use the grain for weighing precious stones and metals. In oriental countries the carob seed was used for centuries as a unit of weight and diamonds, other gems and pearls are still weighed in carats, which is a derivation from the name of the carob seed.

The decimal metric system devised in France gives us the gramme as the unit of weight. Of course in weighing we also

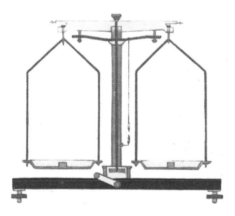

need a range of submultiples and multiples in order to cover very tiny amounts of poisons, medicine, precious stones etc. and enormous quantities, for example, of large animals, machinery and ships.

Why there are some special submultiples

As a result of the great development of science and particularly the rapid progress which has been made during this century, the decimal metric system has had to undergo considerable changes. For example, how would it be possible to measure the infinitely tiny creatures discovered by the electron microscope by means of the normal submultiples? Even the smallest unit, the millimetre, would seem enormous for such purposes.

Special submultiples had therefore to be invented which, although linked with the decimal metric system, provide facilities for further measurement.

The first of these extraordinary submultiples is the micron which is equal to one-millionth of a metre or one-thousandth of a millimetre.

This seems infinitesimal but it is not the smallest unit. Below that is the nanometre, a thousandth-millionth of a metre.

Scientists also indicate very small amounts with two figures connected by a multiplication sign such as 15×10^{-6}. The first figure (15) indicates the number of units. The second figure ($^{-6}$) indicates the size of the unit by giving the number of zeros in it. A minus sign and six zeros indicate that the units are millionths (a million having six zeros). A measurement of 15×10^{-6} metres is therefore 15 millionths of a metre.

To get even a slight idea of the purpose of these exceptional submultiples, it is perhaps useful to remember that bacteria measure a few thousandths of a millimetre and viruses as little as millionths of a millimetre.

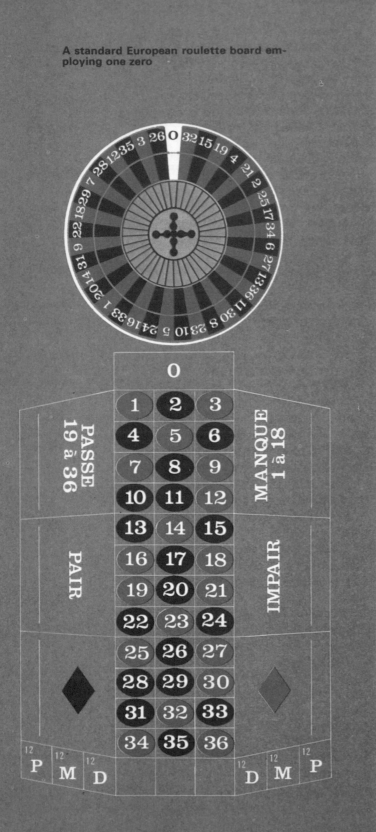

A standard European roulette board employing one zero

Why every house has meters

Few houses today are without electricity and gas. The user of these services has to pay, in addition to a fixed charge, an amount based on the quantity of electricity or gas actually consumed.

Automatic meters are fitted in the houses to measure the amount used by the consumer. For instance, whenever you turn on the gas the meter is operated by the flow of the gas through the pipes. The flow turns a special counter which progressively adds up the amount of gas used. A similar thing happens with electricity. Special inspectors call at every house and read these meters. The value of the amount which has been consumed is then worked out and a bill sent to the consumer.

In some European countries water is also measured in this way. Water meters work in essentially the same way as gas meters.

Why it is difficult to win at roulette

Roulette is a gambling game played in the casinos of Europe and North and South America.

Those who organize casinos are well aware of the theory of probabilities whilst the players seldom or never know much about it; also the bank or casino is able to guard against surprises by various devices.

Let us take a look at a roulette table with its numbers up to thirty-six, that is eighteen black numbers and eighteen red ones, plus nought.

Suppose that we exploit only

the pairs of probabilities: evens and odds, red or black, high or low. To begin with these probabilities are not exactly equal because of the figure nought, one of the devices mentioned, because if the nought comes up everything not on nought is lost except for the even numbers which remain valid for the next turn.

What are the chances of a particular number coming up, including nought? Twice in seventy-four turns, equal to thirty-seven losses, thirty-six wins and one returned. This seems quite an advantage to the player but that small margin is enough to guarantee the bank against surprise.

Why graphs are used

Numbers have always been very useful instruments of human progress but sometimes a great deal of ability and analysis is required to interpret them.

To make certain mathematical and geometrical situations comprehensible to ordinary people without the use of numbers, we use graphs. As the world indicates these are drawings which show in diagram form the stages of an operation, the ratios of a quantity, and so on.

Here are two examples.

If the sales of a business are increasing, the situation will be shown graphically by an oblique sloping line on a background of squares (linear graph).

To give a visual idea of the comparative parts which make up a substance, a circle is drawn divided into segments of different sizes in relation to the amounts they represent (circular graph).

Why computers are necessary in modern war

When weapons were very simple man could use them without the need for any special apparatus. This is no longer the case today when their speed and complexity make automation essential.

Let us take the example of an aerial attack. Two radars follow simultaneously the movements of the enemy supersonic bomber and of the ground-to-air missile launched against it. The signals picked up by the two radars are fed into an electronic computer which works them out and communicates the details of the missile's course to a transmitter which is guiding the missile on to the target.

All this takes place simultaneously, within a split second. How could a man calculate at such speed?

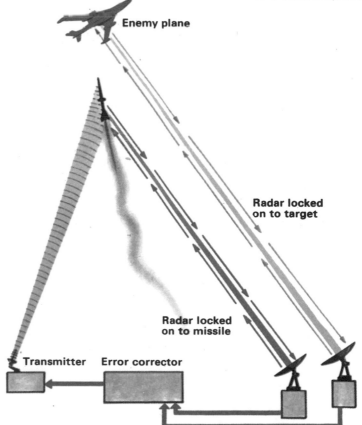

Radio control system

Enemy plane

Radar locked on to target

Radar locked on to missile

Transmitter   Error corrector

THE WHY OF SCIENCE AND TECHNOLOGY

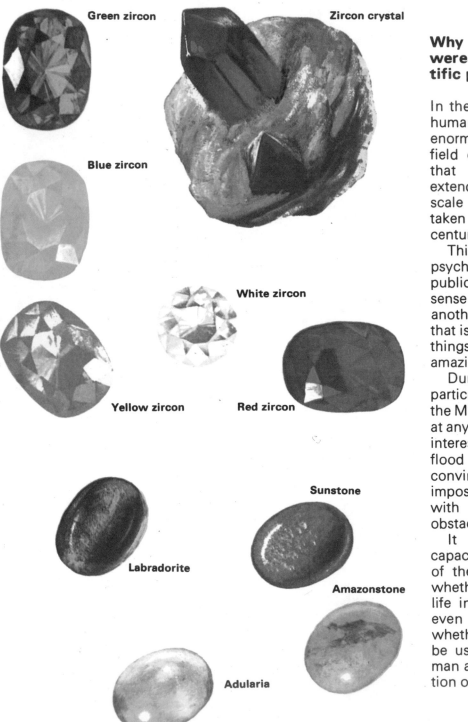

Green zircon

Zircon crystal

Blue zircon

White zircon

Yellow zircon

Red zircon

Labradorite

Sunstone

Amazonstone

Adularia

Why the last two centuries were so important for scientific progress

In the past 150 years the rate of human progress has increased enormously. There is not a single field of science and technology that has not been examined, extended or revised by the large-scale developments which have taken place during the past two centuries.

This phenomenon has caused a psychological reaction among the public in general which in one sense may appear natural but in another sense is quite astonishing; that is the easy acceptance of new things, however unexpected and amazing they may be.

During the past few years and particularly since the conquest of the Moon, people no longer marvel at anything and show scarcely any interest in the ever-increasing flood of inventions. They are convinced that now nothing is impossible to the human mind with its ability to overcome all obstacles and solve all difficulties.

It will depend upon man's capacity for making the best use of the world's natural resources whether we shall have a peaceful life in future, but it will depend even more upon his wisdom whether these resources are to be used for the real progress of man and not for the total destruction of man and his environment.

Why airships are no longer used

As a means of transport airships had their golden age in the early decades of this century, although they originated some fifty years before. It seemed that they might develop to such an extent as to be able to compete with sea transport. But the sudden and tremendous disaster (36 dead) which struck a giant Zeppelin on 6 May 1937 marked the abrupt end of airships, the so-called lighter-than-air machines.

The reason for such a rapid disappearance, which is rare in the world of modern technology, was due to two factors: the lack of safety and the slow speed. Modern aeroplanes offer greater safety and incomparable speed.

Airships built for special purposes appear to have come back again in recent years but it is extremely unlikely that they will ever again be used for passenger transport.

Why in future we shall have to purify sea water

The life of modern man calls for an ever increasing consumption of water. To take one example from industry: to build a single motorcar needs two and a half million litres of water. The situation is just as surprising with regard to food: the maize plant absorbs an average of 200 litres of water for every kilo of seed it produces; for a loaf of bread 3,000 litres of water are required.

However, the world's water reserves cannot increase to meet rising demand for water, and so new ways of obtaining fresh water must be discovered.

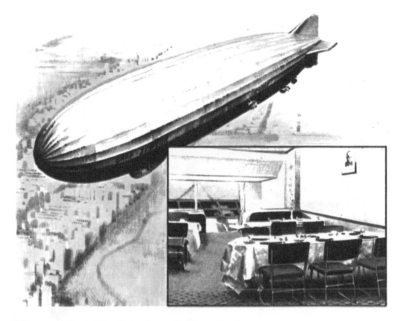

The comfortable interior of the Graf Zeppelin

In contrast to the shortage of water and the increasing demand for it there is the enormous amount of water to be found in the oceans and seas.

There is, therefore, a pressing need to purify sea water. One actual example is Kuwait, where all the fresh water used is obtained by distillation of sea water.

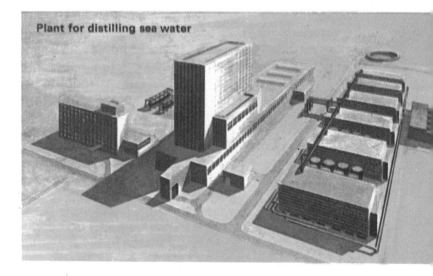

Plant for distilling sea water

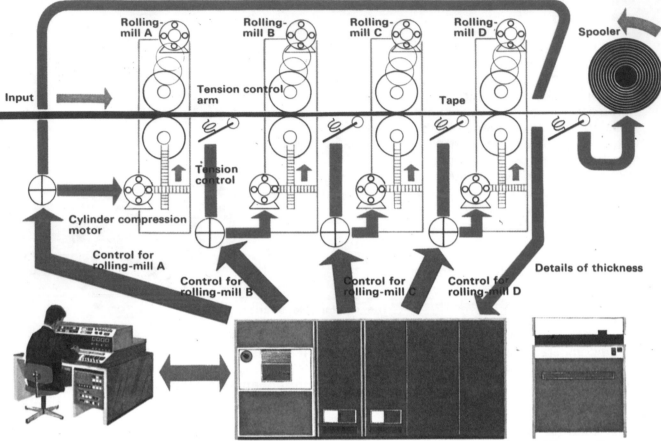

Input · Rolling-mill A · Rolling-mill B · Rolling-mill C · Rolling-mill D · Spooler · Tension control arm · Tape · Tension control · Cylinder compression motor · Control for rolling-mill A · Control for rolling-mill B · Control for rolling-mill C · Control for rolling-mill D · Details of thickness · Operator · Processor · Memory discs

Why man needs electronic computers

The complex structure of modern society, the enormous problems arising from technical and scientific developments, the continuous search for perfection in many fields of industry and numerous other factors all contribute to the need for more and more complicated calculations.

The human mind is able to do all these calculations perfectly well and can resolve the enormous mathematical problems which progress demands, but there is one great drawback: slowness. Extremely complicated operations and calculations would require years of mental work.

Today this work can be carried out quickly and efficiently by machines, the so-called electronic computers. So much has already been achieved by science in this field that the computer has literally invaded every sector of our lives, not only science and technology but also commerce and even political and social life. From air navigation to traffic control, from automation in medicine to automation in factories, from complicated calculations for printing a newspaper to weather forecasts, computers are in constant demand to supply prompt and accurate answers. If we did not have these machines today humanity would have to mark time and the path of progress would be blocked.

Why magnetic trains are being used in some places

Travelling into the centres of large and crowded cities can be a great problem. Unless there is an adequate system of public transport, traffic jams and parked vehicles will block the streets. Buses help to keep private cars off the streets, but the most important means of public city transport is by rail.

These rail networks are mainly underground, but in some cities it is difficult to build new underground railways, either because the ground is not suitable or because the cost of excavating the tunnels is too great. It is in such cases that a new form of public transport may come to people's aid – the magnetic train.

This kind of train has no wheels. It floats just above its track, which may be built on or over the ground, by magnetic levitation. A linear induction motor drives the train along, also using the force of magnetism. Because the train does not actually come into contact with its track, it can move very swiftly. Experimental magnetic trains have reached speeds of 500 kilometres an hour.

A magnetic train contains either electromagnets, which give a powerful magnetic field when fed with electricity, or permanent magnets. These magnets are situated in the track and beneath the train. They act to raise the train above the track and to propel it along the track.

The new magnetic trains are much quieter than other forms of transport and consume less energy. They promise to provide rapid services from airports to city centres as well as fast inter-city services.

Why hovercraft are so successful

Water offers strong resistance to swimmers and vessels of any kind. However powerful the means of propulsion, the speed of a vessel is very limited as compared with land and air transport.

The inventors of the hovercraft had the idea of building a vehicle which could travel on water without being immersed in it. The hovercraft creates a cushion of air which enables it to remain poised slightly above the surface of the water and thus to achieve high speeds. Excellent results have been obtained in trials and hovercraft services now operate on several short sea routes. One service carries passengers and cars across the English Channel.

Although the hovercraft has been developed primarily for use over water, it is also able to travel overland.

Christopher Cockerell who is regarded as the father of the hovercraft, has experimented with rail transport. However, hovertrains have not proved to be practical, and magnetic levitation is now being investigated as a superior method of travel.

Monorail test track of car which can carry 125 people at about 100 k.p.h. (above)

Model of hovercraft on high-speed track, driven by a linear induction motor

Why goods are sent in special containers

Enormous quantities of goods used to be carried in the holds of ships, packed into cases and containers of all shapes and sizes: sacks, bales, baskets, trunks. To embark, stow and disembark all these goods was a very complicated and often tiresome task, due mainly to the large variety of packages. This situation still persists in some cases.

Recently, however, a system of transport has been developed which, because of its rational approach, will very soon revolutionize and replace the old methods.

The idea is to build containers of standard sizes which are common to all countries of the world. These containers are like huge rectangular boxes. There are big ones and smaller ones but made in such a way that the smaller ones can be contained inside the larger.

This apparently very ordinary idea is having important consequences in the field of transport. Special ships have been built with holds designed to accommodate a specified number of containers, like enormous boxes, each exactly the same size as the others. This greatly facilitates trans-shipment with considerable saving of time and effort. Major seaports have undergone massive expansion in order to handle these containers.

Special cranes place the containers in the holds or take them out again in accordance with a very carefully devised programme, perfectly rational and easy to operate.

These containers are used not only for transport by sea, but also by land and by air.

Why the microscope has saved many lives

The microscope is an instrument fitted with special lenses which enables us to see things which are invisible to the naked eye. Before the microscope was invented we were not aware of the existence of the infinite multitude of tiny creatures, the micro-organisms, which play such an important part in our lives.

The microcosm, or the world of the infinitely small, is more populated than one would think. It includes both organisms which are useful to man and some which are harmful and even deadly.

It is in the sphere of microscopic analysis applied to medicine that the microscope has proved to be indispensable. The research work made possible by the microscope determines whether science is able to identify and control those micro-organisms which are harmful to man and to encourage those which are beneficial to him.

All branches of medicine make use of the microscope. For instance, the pathologists, who specialize in discovering the causes of disease, make their diagnoses only after a careful microscopic examination of cell tissue taken from the patients. The best course of medical or surgical action can then be determined.

Bacteriology and microbiology are perhaps the scientific subjects most closely connected with the study of diseases. They could not exist without the microscope as their task is to study the micro-organisms and germs which infect man.

Important discoveries have recently been announced in the study of tumours: it appears that they may be caused by viruses. If these diseases also are to be conquered, it will be due to the microscope which enables us to identify these particular micro-organisms.

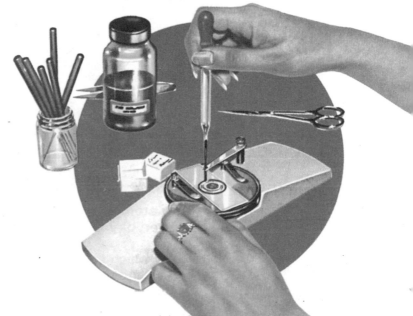

Stereomicroscopes are used in delicate surgery

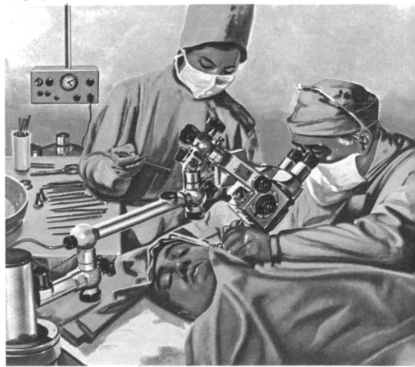

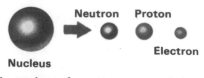

If the nucleus of an atom measured about 1 centimetre in diameter, the whole atom would have a diameter of about 180 metres

All materials whether organic or inorganic are made up of atoms

Why the atom is so important in our everyday lives

Everything which exists in nature, all living creatures and non-living things on the Earth, are composed of atoms.

These tiny particles, infinitely small as they are (their diameter is one hundred millionth part of a centimetre), are of astounding vitality. Each atom is composed of a central nucleus of protons and neutrons around which electrons circle continuously.

Modern science has made a discovery which is destined to have enormous consequences in the life of man. It has been able to split the atom, an action which used to be considered absolutely impossible.

The immediate effect of splitting the atom is the release of the energy it contains. It is therefore possible to obtain energy in colossal quantities by bombarding atoms.

To get some idea, however approximate, of the importance of this phenomenon, let us take just one example: the energy obtained by the breaking down of one kilo of Uranium 235 is equal to that which would be obtained by burning 6 million tons of coal.

The very complex apparatus needed to produce atomic energy is called a nuclear reactor. There are many of these now functioning very well in several countries of the world and more are being built. The electrical energy which they produce is used in a thousand different ways to the benefit of mankind.

Some large naval units are also now driven by atomic energy. Complicated apparatus for distilling sea water also works through nuclear reactors. Many electric power stations convert nuclear energy into electrical energy.

Radio-active isotopes are widely employed in medicine, agriculture and industry. By their help ways are being discovered of fighting disease, substances useful for human nutrition are being discovered and machines are being built of high technical precision and outstanding performance.

Why quasars are studied

Quasars, which were first identified in 1960, emit radio waves as well as light. Measurements of their light show that they are immense distances from us – thousands of millions of light years away. To be detected at such distances, quasars must emit vast amounts of light or radio waves, yet they appear to be little bigger than a star. One solution to this mystery is that quasars are the centres of distant galaxies, and they contain black holes that cause an immense outburst of energy.

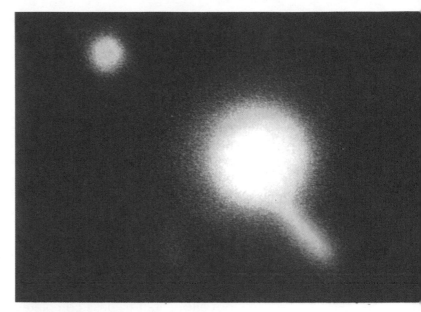

(top) *Quasar* 3C 273

(bottom) **The radiotelescope at Jodrell Bank**

Why radio telescopes are better for observing the most distant stars

Technical and scientific progress first made available to man instruments such as the telescope which enabled astronomers to bring the heavenly bodies nearer and study them more closely.

About fifty years ago, astronomers discovered that it is possible to study heavenly bodies such as stars and galaxies by the radio waves that they send out into space, even as far away as several millions of light years from Earth. What they discovered was, in fact, that many stars relatively near to us, such as the Sun, and many very remote ones send out special radio waves.

To collect these waves and analyse them to obtain precise information is the task of the radio telescopes, that is telescopes which observe by radio the remotest forms of stellar activity. This has increased to an enormous extent the scope of astronomical discovery.

157

Why astronomical observatories are built on high mountains

The planet Earth is surrounded by an enormous layer of air, the atmosphere. It allows light and certain radiations to pass through but presents an impenetrable barrier to a multitude of other radiations which could be harmful to life. Although this is a good thing for us, it is a disadvantage for astronomical research because all cosmic radiation can provide useful scientific information of particular value to astronomy. Moreover, the atmosphere does not allow light to pass completely unhindered partly because the rays of the Sun are often intercepted by clouds and also because there is always some atmospheric dust suspended in the air.

For all these reasons astronomical observatories are built at high levels where the obstacles to the passage of cosmic radiations are greatly reduced.

The Observatory on the Pic du Midi, 2,700 metres in the Pyrenees is one of the highest observatories in the world

Why balloons are used for astronomical research

Astronomers have always wanted observatories situated as high as possible. It was a great step forward when astronomical observatories were built on high mountains and a further decisive step was taken a few years ago when special balloons were used to carry limited astronomical instruments up to the higher strata of the atmosphere.

These astronomical balloons were made of a waterproof outer covering and usually contained either hydrogen or helium. Helium is the most used because hydrogen could easily burst into flames if it comes into contact with oxygen, which exists in large quantities in the atmosphere. Indeed, hydrogen and oxygen form a highly inflammable and explosive mixture. Both hydrogen and helium are gases which are lighter than air and therefore balloons containing them tend to rise to great heights, even as much as 40,000 metres.

The instruments which these balloons carried up to such heights were able to collect a great deal of information which it would be impossible to obtain at ground level. These balloons have been gradually improved until today they are very useful and sometimes even indispensable research instruments.

New possibilities are opening up for astronomical science as a result of the development of artificial satellites that orbit the Earth in space high above the atmosphere. These astronomical satellites, which include the space telescope due to be launched in 1986, send their observations back to the ground by radio.

Why we sometimes see rainbows in the sky

Generally we have little idea of light, particularly that of the Sun. The most we think of is that it is useful for life on Earth.

However, light is a natural phenomenon with some very interesting features. It has an impressive speed of almost 300,000 kilometres a second, covers particular wave lengths and is the sum of all the colours it contains.

As well as in the laboratory, the composition of light can also be studied in the sky under certain natural conditions. We see, for instance, a rainbow in the sky which displays all the wonderful colours of the spectrum. What has happened? Millions of drops of water, on which the Sun's rays are falling, act like an enormous prism and break the light up into its component colours. That is why a rainbow frequently appears after a storm.

Why intercontinental television is possible

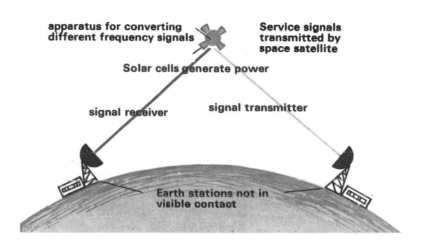

apparatus for converting different frequency signals

Service signals transmitted by space satellite

Solar cells generate power

signal receiver

signal transmitter

Earth stations not in visible contact

Television waves travel in straight lines and cannot be reflected from the ionosphere like radio waves. To transmit television programmes between continents separated by oceans it is not possible to erect in the middle of the seas the booster aerials necessary for the propagation of television waves.

The problem was brilliantly solved by means of artificial satellites which have been placed in a stationary orbit around the Earth at a distance of thousands of kilometres. They are fitted out for the purpose of receiving and retransmitting television signals.

Why the first cars had solid tyres

When a technical discovery is made and something new is produced it is based logically upon ideas and materials which already exist.

This is what happened to the motor car. At first it was really a coach in which the engine replaced the horse as the motive power. It had the same shape, the same hood, the same cover, the same steps for getting in and out and, of course, the same wheels and the same solid tyres.

The reason for the solid tyres is simply that pneumatic tyres had not yet been invented. They were invented by John Boyd Dunlop, a Belfast veterinary surgeon, in the year 1887. It was a rubber tube containing compressed air for the purpose of mitigating the shocks the vehicle received on the roads which in those days were particularly rough. Pneumatic tyres were first invented for bicycles but were very soon fitted to every type of vehicle, except, of course, trains.

Why balloons must have means of rising and descending quickly

The force of ascension of balloons is given, in accordance with the principle of Archimedes, by the difference between the weight of the mass of air displaced by the envelope and the weight of the gas contained in the balloon. Balloons are in fact lighter-than-air machines. Whilst it is relatively easy to make these machines rise, it is very difficult to control them when they are in flight. To make them rise or descend at the wish of the pilot is sometimes a rather tricky undertaking. During navigation balloons are subjected to uncontrollable forces. For instance condensation of water vapour or ice may form on the envelope, there may be escapes of gas or gusts of wind. In these circumstances, to ascend or descend may mean the difference between safety and mortal danger for the crew. Methods have therefore been studied to allow quick changes of height. Two devices are of particular importance: a rip cord on the balloon to provide quick release of gas in case of emergency, and a load of ballast, usually sand, which can be jettisoned to lighten the machine and cause it to rise.

Why James Watt was a pioneer of the industrial age

The steam engine originated in England early in the eighteenth century.

At that time two patents were taken out for atmospheric pressure steam engines but their use was confined to pumping water and they had a number of working faults.

It was left to James Watt, a Scottish instrument maker, to perfect the steam engine by a device which was both simple and decisive: the condenser ensured that the steam engine could continue to run without loss of pressure. After much experiment Watt patented his improvements in 1769.

From that moment the most varied applications of steam engines to industrial machines became possible.

In 1781 Watt built the first large scale steam engine which he later improved still further.

Why the first trains were drawn by steam engines

The first types of true motor cars were steam engines applied to vehicles. This fact alone would not have guaranteed them against competition by other kinds of motors if, as far as the railways are concerned, locomotives had not immediately proved to be such powerful and practical engines able to meet any demand. Even the most sceptical individuals were soon convinced. In forty years England had passed from the few kilometres of the Liverpool-Manchester railway of 1830 to almost 22,000 kilometres in 1870.

No other engine could compete with the steam engine although as early as 1879 the first electric locomotive had appeared but it was very small. The first English electric railway was opened on 3 August 1883. However steam engines dominated the scene for many years and are still in use on some railways.

Why aerodynamic shape is important in vehicles

Any body which moves in a gas or liquid has its movement conditioned by its shape: if it is squat it will be slowed down and if it is slender it will be speeded up. The slender shape of a body which is intended to move at speed through the air is more correctly called aerodynamic, that is a shape which offers the least resistance to the air.

Nature provides us with many examples of aerodynamic shapes; the commonest is that of birds. Man, the eternal copier of nature, gave aerodynamic shape to weapons he hurled at a distance, lances and arrows which were pointed not only to penetrate the flesh of animals but also to be able to pass more quickly through the air.

As for transport, right from the very beginning man made all his boats slender, but for land vehicles the problem of aerodynamics only arose with the invention of the motor car. The first real aerodynamic motor car goes back to 1899 when the Belgian inventor Camille Jenatzy had the idea that a slimmer shape would reduce air resistance and would make his car, which he had called *Jamais Contente*, much faster.

Why wind tunnels are used

Almost all parts of aeroplanes are subjected to strong, often very strong pressures from the air through which they move. To take a common example: the wings of aeroplanes have to support very high pressures during flight as they cleave their way through the air. That is why aircraft designers and builders have to identify as accurately as possible all the places most subject to stress, so that they can be suitably strengthened or provided with special equipment.

As it would be impossible to study, analyse and observe accurately the behaviour during motion or flight, tunnels have been built in which the natural conditions of flight can be reproduced artificially. These tunnels are fitted with special devices which can control the velocity, temperature and pressure of the currents of air which blow through them.

In the test chamber the aeroplane, or the part of it which is to be studied, is completely stationary and can therefore be observed easily and minutely when it is under stress from the artificial flow of air which recreates the conditions of flight.

Thanks to this device many constructional faults have been found and corrected. Special structures have been devised suitable for high speeds and new aerodynamic techniques have been discovered.

The use of wind tunnels in research has not been limited to aeronautics. Aerodynamic studies on trains, boats and cars have been carried out and the effect of wind pressure on buildings and bridges has also been tested.

Why the electric car is not in everyday use

The air of the large cities is being polluted to the incredible but true extent of 90 per cent by the exhaust gases of motor cars fitted with internal combustion engines. In Los Angeles it has been estimated that the production of carbon monoxide exceeds 10 million kilogrammes daily, 80 per cent of which is due to petrol exhaust fumes.

Electrically propelled vehicles, on the other hand, are very clean, that is to say that they do not give off gases and are not therefore harmful to people or the atmosphere.

You may think that electrically driven vehicles are something new: This is not so and according to the opinion of many experts they were the first of all self-propelled vehicles.

The first automobile was built by a man called Davidson in England in 1842. It was an electric carriage and was moved by means of eight electromagnets operated by batteries.

More surprising still is the fact that many records have been broken by electric cars. On 18 December 1898 the *Jeantaud* electric car reached the considerable speed of 63 kilometres an hour. This was only the first victory. A few months later, on 29 April 1899, another electrically driven car exceeded 100 kilometres an hour; it was the *Jamais Contente*, the name of which is a promise of further victories.

Why then, after such a fine start, were electric cars so heavily outclassed by petrol engined cars? There are two reasons: weight and cost.

The first reason is certainly the more serious. The batteries for supplying the energy to the electric motor have to be made of materials which are very heavy and also can only be used for a few hours at a time. When we add to this the high cost, we can see why electric vehicles are used only for certain services, in railway stations and mines but not on the roads. This does not mean that the most serious disadvantages may not be overcome in the future and enable electric cars to be more widely used. It would be a good thing for us all.

Why steel is only a recent invention

When we recall that man discovered metals in prehistoric times, the era of steel which goes back less than 150 years may seem quite recent. Before then cast iron,

In modern steel mills production is planned, co-ordinated and controlled by computers

which was brittle, and wrought iron, which was too soft, were the main construction materials.

It is universally agreed that the father of steel was Henry Bessemer, an English engineer. Just a century ago at a meeting of the British Association which is now famous, he announced the beginning of the steel era in a lecture entitled 'The processing of forged iron and steel without fuel'.

Steel was already in use at the time of Bessemer and he did not, therefore, invent this alloy. However, at that time the methods of producing steel were very inefficient. They took a long time and were very expensive and for the most part the steel was of very poor quality. There was a growing demand for a strong, tough, wear-resistant metal that could be produced at an economic price.

The process invented by Bessemer and known as the converter process combined extreme simplicity of construction and operation with a perfect product. It is still widely used and consists essentially of a container capable of holding 5 to 15 tons of material, the shape of which is something like the old alchemist's retort, but of huge size. Made of sheet metal and lined with refractory material, the converter is able to rotate around a horizontal axis located a little above its centre of gravity. Air is introduced through this axis for the purpose of oxidizing the material and liberating the excess carbon contained in the cast iron and in the silicon and manganese.

Because the Bessemer converter is able to refine the cast iron in the molten state, it enables large amounts of steel to be produced with any desired carbon content.

Why artificial satellites do not fall back on to the Earth

First of all we must make a distinction with regard to artificial satellites. Properly speaking satellites are those devices which are launched into space by means of rocket carriers and put into orbit around the Earth. Space probes are those which are launched towards other planets in the solar system.

Some artificial satellites placed in low orbit either deliberately or in error are seriously impeded by the residual atmosphere and may be retarded to such an extent as to fall back towards the Earth. However, these satellites usually burn up in the atmosphere and do not reach the ground.

How are satellites able to orbit the Earth? The rocket that launches a satellite accelerates it to a high speed at a great height above the Earth. The satellite will then continue to move around the Earth, taking up an orbit dictated by the speed, height and direction in which it is launched, and unless it is subsequently retarded by traces of the Earth's atmosphere at low orbits, the satellite will continue to travel through space indefinitely. However, the satellite does not escape the Earth's gravitational field, and this is the factor that pulls it into a circular or elliptical orbit around the Earth.

So far the answer is a simple one but it becomes more difficult when we ask where these satellites will finish up. Since October 1957, when the Russians launched *Sputnik I*, countless artificial satellites have been put into orbit around the Earth. Control of some of them was lost very soon and others carried on their work for years.

Why so many artificial satellites have been put into orbit

After discovering the method of placing artificial satellites in orbit around the Earth and of launching them towards other planets of the solar system, scientists began to examine ways in which such a promising invention could be used.

Satellites can be divided into two types: those which are purely for scientific purposes and those which are used for military and warlike objectives. Among the first is the famous *Explorer I* to which we owe a fundamental discovery regarding cosmic radiation. It was by this means that the American scientist Van Allen discovered the radiations which could have had a tragic effect on those taking part in space flights. Just as famous because of the immediate effect it had throughout the world is *Telstar* which made possible the first transatlantic television.

Today there are very many such satellites equipped for meteorological research, for astronomical studies and for communication. Only the future can reveal how many more fields of research and public use will be benefited by the artificial statellites.

Why iron can float on water

Ships are built of iron and yet they do not sink. Why is this? The explanation was given by Archimedes of Syracuse, a scientist who lived more than 2,000 years ago. He stated the principle like this: a body immersed in a liquid is subject to an upward thrust equal to the weight of the volume of liquid displaced. This thrust is the sum of the pressures which the liquid exerts on the surface of the body.

Archimedes' principle is valid whether the body is completely immersed, like a submarine, or only partly immersed, like surface vessels.

Shipbuilders have to keep this principle in mind if they do not want their ships to go to the bottom when they are launched, which has sometimes happened. In order to obtain an upward thrust sufficient to keep the ship afloat, they have to calculate very accurately the amount of liquid which the vessel will displace when it is in the water.

Iron can therefore float given certain conditions. It can also rise and float again when it has been immersed. This is what happens with submarines. To make

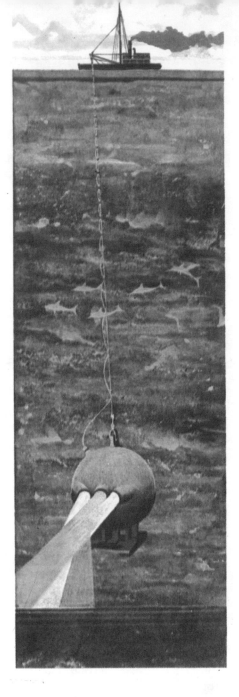

them sink certain tanks are opened so that they fill with water. This increases the weight of the vessel so as to overcome the thrust of the water, that is the weight of the displaced liquid.

To rise again, the opposite action is required; the water is blown out of the tanks and the vessel becomes lighter.

Why it is very difficult to explore the depths of the sea

The exploration of the ocean depths has always had a fascination for man and there have been many daring attempts even though some of them met with little success.

The greatest obstacle has always been that of weight and the pressure of the water. The deeper a body sinks the more it is crushed by the pressure and beyond a certain depth the pressure

Why a balloon bursts if it rises too high

Atmospheric pressure varies according to temperature, wind and latitude and in particular it varies with height: the higher you go, the less the pressure because there is less air above you.

It we take a rubber balloon and fill it with gas, which is lighter than air, it will tend to rise from the ground.

If we release it, it will rise to a considerable height but there may

is really colossal.

Scientists and technicians are therefore making constant efforts to build hulls which will withstand greater pressures.

Another obstacle is that of the difficulties of moving. For example bathyspheres, the steel spheres used in underwater exploration, are suspended on a cable attached to a boat and so their range of action is very limited.

come a time when it will burst. That is because there has been a change in the ratio between the internal pressure of the balloon and the reduced pressure of the atmosphere around it. When the internal pressure is greater than the external pressure, the balloon begins to swell still more until it bursts.

Balloons have been used in scientific research, war and sports.

Why electrical charges form in the sky

The clouds which mass in the sky before a storm become charged with electricity through passing over strata of air at different temperatures. As a general rule positive charges prevail at high cloud levels and negative charges at low levels.

When the heavily charged

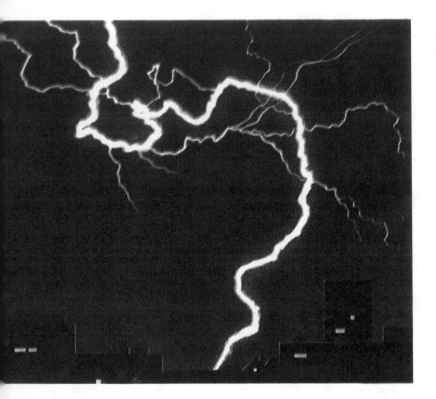

clouds descend towards the Earth, the latter, through the phenomenon of induction, becomes charged with electricity of opposite sign. Two electromagnetic fields, often of very great extent, are thus formed. At this point the negative charges are strongly impelled to discharge towards the positive charges, because opposite charges attract one another. However the air offers a strong obstacle to the passage of electrical charges as

it is not a good conductor of electricity. It undergoes a rapid process of ionization which creates conditions which permit the passage of electricity. An infinity of minute electrical charges erupt through the ionized zones in perfect and rapid succession but we see them as one long, forked and twisted discharge. We call it lightning.

Lightning passes not only from the clouds to the Earth, but also in the opposite direction, and goes, too, from cloud to cloud, although this is rare. It is often followed by that other phenomenon, thunder.

Why electricity is transmitted at high tension

The use of electricity has reached enormous proportions. Consequently there arose a need to transport electricity to ever greater distances. This raised a serious problem. Direct current had to be transmitted at the output voltage of the dynamo which produced it, but because of the electrical resistance of the wires along which it passed there was a considerable drop in the voltage after a short distance. This meant that some of the power was lost along the way. It was not possible to reduce the resistance by increasing the thickness of the wire as this would have made the wires impossibly large and heavy.

To overcome these losses, the use of alternating current was introduced, as alternating current can be transported at the desired high voltages.

As the loss of power of electrical energy during its passage along wires is caused by the amount of current and as the carrying potential is equal to the current multiplied by the tension, we are able by increasing the tension to transport large amounts of current using relatively thin wires.

At the points where the electricity is to be used suitable transformers are connected to reduce the voltage to a less dangerous level, such as 240 volts which is normal for domestic use in Britain.

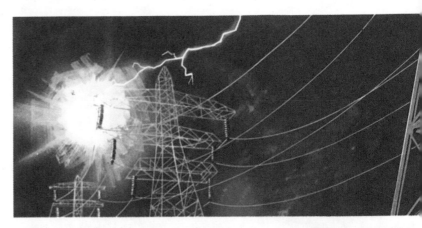

Why electric current does not pass from the wires to the metal pylons

The huge pylons which carry the electric cables are a normal sight today. These pylons are made of steel and are able to carry high tension electric cables without themselves being affected by the current.

This is due to special insulators. One of these for use with high tension is the bell-shaped insulator. It is made of tempered glass or porcelain and is used in series of ten or more. The various insulators are fitted with metal connecting bolts and hooks for fastening at the top to the pylon brackets and at the bottom to the conducting cable.

Because of the way it is built the series of bell insulators is able to yield to the force of the wind without any risk of damage to the cables. The insulators are fitted with special arresters which absorb the effects of any lightning that may strike the line. As the dust which settles on the insulators could, if covered with rain water, become a conductor of electricity, each insulator has special collars fitted in such a way as to increase the distance for any possible short circuits.

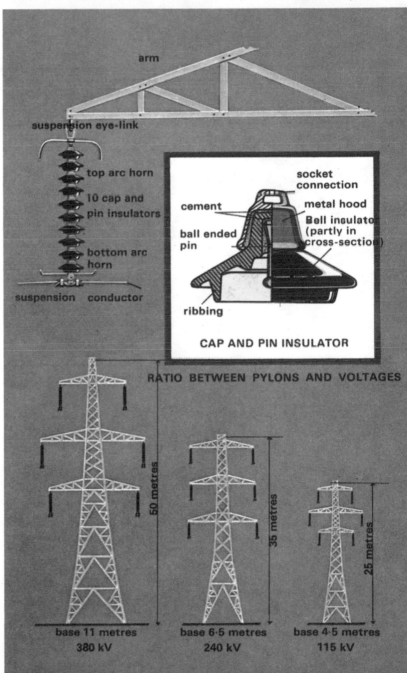

arm

suspension eye-link

top arc horn

10 cap and pin insulators

bottom arc horn

suspension conductor

cement

socket connection

metal hood

ball ended pin

Bell insulator (partly in cross-section)

ribbing

CAP AND PIN INSULATOR

RATIO BETWEEN PYLONS AND VOLTAGES

50 metres

35 metres

25 metres

base 11 metres
380 kV

base 6·5 metres
240 kV

base 4·5 metres
115 kV

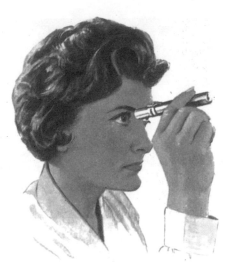

Special instruments exist for measuring radioactivity and they are used particularly by those employed in nuclear power stations

extend the complicated work of research to an ever larger number of individuals, educated for this purpose by years of serious study.

There are many and various reasons for this changed situation with regard to scientific research. First it is easy to see what a decisive part it plays in all our lives. Just think, for instance, of the survival of certain populations which could be achieved by more progressive agriculture; think of the fight against disease; of the enormous possibilites on the still untouched natural resources. Secondly, the advance of science has produced problems of such enormity that they can only be solved by a colossal and collective research effort.

Why so much money is invested in atomic research

Among the numerous fields of study in which science is at present engaged, atomic research undoubtedly offers the greatest possibilities. This is not only because it is a relatively new and largely unexplored field but also because of the vast potential. There is practically nothing that will not be affected for good or ill by this science. and yet it is only about forty years ago that its destructive power was first revealed to the world.

It is because of the great possibilities of atomic science that every day more and more capital is used to finance studies, research and experiments in the nuclear field. This is not by the great world powers only, but also by countries of much smaller economic potential.

If all the efforts expended in this field could be directed to peaceful

Why scientific research is important

The great scientific discoveries which have brought mankind to its present state of progress in almost every sphere were in the past always the result of individual research.

But today in every field of culture and particularly in science and technology there is a need to aims, it would lead to a truly astonishing contribution to human progress, with all the benefits which such a common effort would achieve.

Unfortunately there still exists among the individual countries a rooted sense of jealousy with regard to discoveries, improvements and inventions. This not only retards universal advancement but also leads to very much higher expenditure of time energy and money.

Why do nations accept such an expenditure? For safety. The power which atomic energy is able to release can be used for warlike purposes and this leads to secrecy on both sides, which it is difficult to overcome.

Why radioactive substances are dangerous

The human body like that of all living creatures is normally able to withstand natural radiations, such as the rays of the Sun, without the risk of any irreparable damage. However, it can suffer serious injury if subjected to artificial radiation such as that produced by man whether for peaceful or warlike purposes. The cells of the body can be destroyed or made inefficient and progressive disintegration can be induced. This happens when radiation affects more or less violently the intimate structure of the living cells, which follow precise natural laws.

Particularly harmful is the damage which artificial radiation can cause to the chromosomes contained in the nuclei of the cells. These may be split and remain divided or may combine with other split chromosomes. In this case the natural genetic con-

sequences become very serious.

Although experiments carried out on guinea-pigs and plants are not yet decisive it seems certain that artificial nuclear radiations have a direct effect on the immediate life of living creatures and on the conditions of reproduction.

Why detectors of radioactive particles are important

The techniques of nuclear science have led to the invention of various instruments for detecting the presence of radiation and to indicate their exact intensity. These detectors or counters, such as the

Handling radioisotopes

well-known Geiger counter, have many applications. Among the most important is the search for radioactive materials: such counters are essential for locating mining areas suitable for intensive exploitation.

Of vital importance also is another application of detectors, that of revealing excess radiation, which is harmful to human beings. Excess radiation can occur in research establishments, laboratories and hospitals.

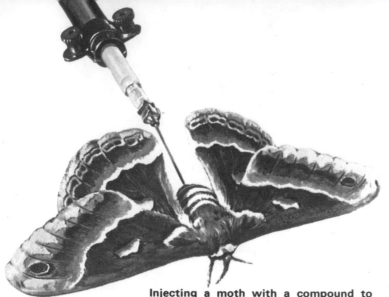

Injecting a moth with a compound to study insect metabolism

Why radioisotopes are used in agriculture

Radioactive isotopes or radio-isotopes are used in very many scientific fields. In agriculture they have been used in research which has produced some surprising results.

The study of fertilizers and the metabolism of minerals in plants, for instance, has been carried out in this way, and so, too, has the measurement of the consumption of phosphorus by plants. In the biochemical field studies of animal metabolism have led to improve-

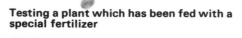

Testing a plant which has been fed with a special fertilizer

ments in animal feeding and increased meat production.

Nuclear science is also waging a decisive battle against plant parasites.

Why radioisotopes will solve the problem of parasites

Every day the fight against parasites is becoming more intense. Enormous areas of cultivated land can be damaged irreparably in a few hours by a massive attack by harmful insects. Traditional methods seem to have little effect and their most serious limitation is that they risk harming nature and destroying the ecological balance which is essential to man's survival.

The method of sterilizing the male insects appears to give good results. This process is based on a principle which it is easy to state but delicate and difficult to put into practice. It consists in breeding a huge quantity of insects of the species it is wished to weaken and to sterilize them by means of special radiations just before they reach maturity. When they are set free in the disinfestation zone, the males mate with the females which have lived in freedom but there are no offspring. By this means the species is destroyed in the areas where it is most prolific. Very successful trials of this method of sterilizing the males have been carried out on the island of Capri against the fruit fly which was seriously affecting the orange crop.

Radioactive isotopes can also be used in the fight against insects which devour the crops in storehouses. Controlled radiations either sterilize or kill the insects without any damage or contamination of the crops themselves.

Why radioisotopes are indispensable in industry

There are a surprising number of uses in industry for radioisotopes: even the expert has to make considerable efforts to keep up to date in a changing field of research and application. In fact not a single day goes by without new roads opening up for the use of radioisotopes in industry. Yet it was only in the 1950s that the industrial applications of radioisotopes began.

Gamma ray radiography is now widely used for checking the welding of pipes in long oil pipelines and radioisotopes also facilitate the discovery of leakages. Radioisotope instruments are used in industry in connection with packaging to determine the exact thickness of cardboard and polythene waterproof containers.

Other types of measurements based on the same principle are used to control the production of a very wide range of synthetic materials.

By means of the gamma rays reflected from glazed surfaces special instruments measure not only the thickness of the varnish itself but also of the tube beneath. By similar means the thickness of rust or corrosion which has occured inside the tubes or pipes can be measured.

To ascertain whether hermetically sealed containers are full and up to what level, once again radioactive isotope instruments are used.

Likewise the thickness of cast metal in the furnaces during the normal process of production can be checked by means of gamma rays from Cobalt 60 and the same process is used to check the thickness of glass in the glass furnaces.

Use of radioisotopes for measuring corrosion within a tube

Machine wear has no secrets from instruments designed to reveal it. It is even possible today to measure the wear of a car's gears when the vehicle has only run a few yards.

Such devices save a great deal of research work and therefore reduce considerably the cost of production.

For measuring impurities in materials, particularly in delicate materials, instruments are used which are able to detect the presence of impurities in the proportion of one in one hundred thousand million parts.

When we remember that nuclear energy is still in its infancy and that we have a long way to go in this direction, we might even say that for good or ill our future will depend on this wonderful force of nature which man has appropriated.

Why solar energy will be widely used in future

The vast amount of energy which the Sun radiates has not yet been exploited on a scientific scale, except to an insignificant degree.

The Sun can be regarded as an enormous thermonuclear reactor and could be of value to man to an extent which can scarcely be imagined today.

In 1955 an international association called the Solar Energy Society was founded for the purpose of promoting research into the Sun and the best methods of utilizing solar radiation.

There are three main ways of harnessing the Sun's power. Solar furnaces contain mirrors that focus the Sun's heat rays on a power-producing unit such as an electric generator. The solar power plant *Solar 1* in California has nearly 2,000 mirrors and generates enough electricity for 6,000 people.

Solar heating panels that are fitted on the roofs of houses absorb the Sun's heat rays and use them to warm water circulating through pipes in the panels.

Solar cells contain materials that generate electricity when struck by sunlight. Spacecraft have panels of solar cells.

Why helicopters are so common nowadays

The helicopter, the latest addition in the field of aeronautics, is today being used more and more in a great variety of activities.

Its chief value is its versatility: it combines some of the features typical of lighter-than-air machines with the normal properties of aeroplanes. A decisive factor is its ability to take off and to land vertically, which means that it can manoeuvre in a very small space. This enables it to be used in an extremely wide range of very varied conditions; rescue work in inaccessible places such as mountains, glaciers, tiny islands, traffic jams; rapid rate of travel so that helicopters can act as an air bridge in emergency situations; low flying at slow speed so that they can be used for the spraying of trees and crops.

**Solar cells
generate power**

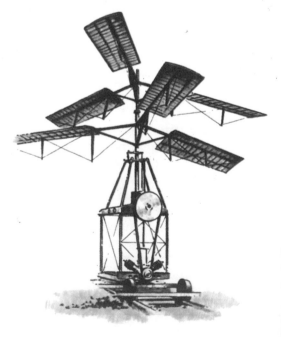

Why it is useful to build nuclear icebreakers

The first naval vessel to use nuclear energy for propulsion was the American submarine *Nautilus* launched in 1955. Today naval ships driven by nuclear power are quite numerous and belong to the great world powers who use them mainly for military purposes. One of the first merchant ships with nuclear propulsion was the *Savannah* which came into service in 1962.

The problem of using such ships for commercial purposes is whether they are useful from an economic point of view. Some aspects in their favour are the fast cruising speed, the infrequent need for refuelling and the capacity of the holds. The disadvantage is the very high cost of nuclear reactors.

Of the non-military naval vessels the most economic are the icebreakers. An outstanding example is the *Lenin* which, by piloting Soviet ships through the ice of the Arctic Ocean, provides a considerable saving of time and money. Without it the same vessels travelling from Murmansk to Vladivostock would have had to go via Suez, a difference of about 14,000 kilometres.

Why port facilities will very soon have to be renewed

Only a few years ago through the initiative of the Japanese ship-building industry, special giant oil tankers were built.

In the early 1960s the first tankers of more than 100,000 tons appeared but today supertankers of over 500,000 tons have become a reality which no longer arouses surprise. Even these may well be exceeded in future.

Their vast size is creating serious problems, for the ports at which these vessels call were built to deal with much smaller ships.

Port equipment for merchant vessels will have to be completely redesigned to facilitate bulk loading and discharging.

The problem of such huge vessels, especially those which carry valuable cargoes, is also made more pressing by political factors such as the closing of the Suez Canal, which occurred during the 1970s as a result of military conflict. Because ships could no longer use the canal, oil tankers were made larger to carry cargoes profitably over longer routes. However, the future of these enormous vessels is now uncertain as oil prices fluctuate.

Why trains need rails

Trains were born on rails and still continue to run on them. This association of trains and rails is due to the way in which trains evolved.

In both the days of horse-drawn vehicles and steam engines the great need was to eliminate friction as much as possible. The growth of the railways and the increased traffic on them increased the importance of the rails which made the railways a safe, fast and comfortable means of travel.

There has been steady and constant progress from cast-iron rails, which wore out very quickly, to iron rails and finally to steel rails.

Today the rails are manufactured in long lengths and are connected together in such a way that the rumbling which used to be a feature of the old rails has been removed.

Why automatic signals are used on the railways

With the ever increasing speeds of the trains and the continued development of the tracks it became necessary to have a system of distant signals, both day and night, which could give a guarantee of safety. That is why the light and sound signals which we know today were installed.

But to make railway travel safer, it was soon realized that it was necessary to provide the railways with an automatic signalling system, both in the stations and on the trains. Indeed, when you think of the number of trains which are dealt with by the large stations, the complexity of the instruments on modern railways and natural difficulties such as fog, landslides and avalanches, you can see how essential an automatic signalling system must be.

Why some aircraft are called supersonic

A supersonic aircraft is one that can fly faster than the speed of sound. This speed is about 1,200 kilometres an hour at sea level, but less

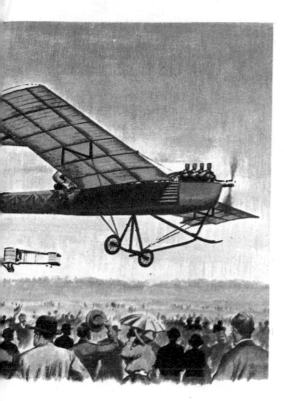

Why aircraft are able to fly

Man has always dreamed of being able to fly but it was not until quite recent times that this dream was fulfilled, first by lighter-than-air machines such as balloons and airships, and then by heavier-than-air machines or aeroplanes driven by airscrews or jet engines. Aeroplanes are able to leave the ground because they can overcome the force of the Earth's gravity. It does not matter whether they are propeller driven or jet machines; what does matter is that the thrust must be great enough to overcome the force of gravity. If, for instance, during flight the engine of an aeroplane stalls and the propulsion ceases, the plane will then fall to the ground.

Flight is therefore movement; immobility is not permitted for heavier-than-air machines.

at high altitudes. The fastest jet fighters can fly at three times the speed of sound. *Concorde*, the supersonic airliner, travels at just over twice the speed of sound.

If you were underneath a supersonic aircraft, you would hear a sharp bang as it passed overhead. The reason that you do not hear these supersonic booms is that aircraft do not normally fly at supersonic speeds over land in case the booms cause damage.

When an aircraft reaches the speed of sound, the sound that it produces travels through the air at the same speed as the aircraft. A strong shock wave builds up at the nose of the aircraft, causing a boom when it reaches the ground. This shock wave could be violent enough to damage the aircraft, but supersonic aircraft have narrow bodies and swept-back wings so that they remain inside the shock wave.

List of Questions

The illustrations in this book are the work of the following artists:
D. Andrews, J. Baker, H. Barnett, J. Batchelor, M. Battersby, J. Bavosi, J.
Beswick, R. S. Coventry, G. Davies, Design Bureau, Design Practitioners Ltd,
G. J. Galsworthy, R. Geary, G. Green, H. Green, R. Hargreaves, N. W. Hearn,
V. Ibbett, K. Lilly, D. MacDougal, A. McBride, M. McGuinness, P. Morter, J.
Nicholls, K. Ody, A. Oxenham, P. Oxenham, G. Palmer, J. Parker, H. Perkins,
D. Pratt, J. Rignall, B. Robertshaw, M. Shoebridge, J. Smith, B. Stallion,
G. Thompson, P. Thornley, C. Tora, D. A. Warner, P. Warner, M. Whittlesea,
Whitecroft Designs Ltd, J. W. Wood, and Associates, W. Wright, E. Wrigley,
M. Youens.